Fiction of Value ———————————————————————

Fiction of Value
Shmulik Fishman

ISBN 978 0 557 388523
Shmulik Fishman
Hampshire College
© 2010

Item 1: A History of Money [1]

I.

There is a common story told to those who are studying money. It is one of an ordinary town with conventional people that have basic needs; they use money for humble purposes. Typically the simulation is told like this:

---

1. Randall Wray states, in his 1998 publication Understanding Modern Money: The Key to Full Employment and Price Stability, that "...It is of course impossible to present an adequate 'history of money' in one chapter." I do not wish to argue with Professor Wray, but I do wish to assert that all histories are stylized and that even a magnum-opus on monetary history would have missing elements and editorial in lieu of fact. This section is meant to drive a point, as all historical articles aim to do. Professor Wray would also take issue with the version of history that I present - that money has evolved from a system of barter to one of symbolic exchange. I will speak to Professor Wray's concerns in Item 2 of this work.

In the community of Capitalville all residents awake each morning to the sound of a helicopter circling above their homes. It's money-hour and each resident quickly goes outside to catch their own set of twenty $20 bills. In Capitalville every resident is employed; after collecting earnings each Capitalvillean begins their daily labor, which pays a living-rate salary.

This adapted version of Milton Friedman's 1969 "helicopter scenario" delivers both an indulgent fantasy - for if only we could have a relationship with such a helicopter - and a gripping reality: money is alluring because it is limited, because money comes in installments. For even in this simulation these residents must budget their spending - setting money aside for, among other items: taxes, monthly bills, groceries and transportation costs. While there are obvious problems with Friedman's scenario,[2] what governs his simulation is an understanding of the function of money that parallels with the present capitalist moment; money acts as the facilitator of a robust system of exchange. However, even with money as the basic element of an economy, Friedman would deemphasize the power that a "money helicopter" would have over a civilization.

Friedman would argue that a Capitalvillean's ephemeral spending binge would be temporary - that such an influx of currency would not have lasting effects because commodity prices would rise to account for this *new* consumer budget. The de-facto economic rationale behind such a claim is that if all receive the same additional quantity of money each day, the effect is void. The conclusion of such a statement, for neoclassical monetary theorists

---

2. One is the question around how and where the helicopter picks up the money it will be delivering if not from the central bank of Capitalville. Many more can be listed or discussed in response to Friedman's problematic scenario and they will be elucidated over the course of this work.

like Friedman, is that money is nothing more then a veil for the real economic activity within a society - that money changes nothing.

What is unarguable is that money and trade are inseparable. Money acts as the facilitator in the exchange of equivalents and, theoretically, Friedman's helicopter should provide aid to the process of exchange. But the helicopter does not arrest the inherent drive that is contained in a typical capitalist society. Sustained is the profit motive, the accumulation of wealth and the reality that capitalists will be controlling the means of production while commanding a winning share of Capitalville's money supply.

There are multiple alterations that can be made to such a simulation in an effort to further display the inner workings of money, but an important one at this juncture would be to change the helicopter's delivery to an unlimited amount of money - in essence a "blank check". In this scenario the monetary market of Capitalville would fail. And for one reason alone: if a helicopter makes money limitless then the monetary value of all commodities would be rendered irrelevant.

II.

Modern paper money is not meant to create value, it is meant to provide a container for it. In a Marxist line of thought, value is derived from the process of creation - from the unique input of human labor.[3] This argument, that all valuable commodities[4] are produced using human hands, is not necessarily

---

3. Marx, 1867, *Capital*.
4. It is important at the outset to establish a clear definition for the term "commodity". *Commodities* are consumable articles that are produced by human labor as a product for sale in the market. A *widget* or *object* is no different from a commodity except that these terms imply an increased level of abstraction and indistinguishability between the commodity in question and other commodities. As posited by Georg Simmel, discussed in the text shortly, the sheer volume of commodities presently in circulation enforces a blasé attitude towards all commodities - decreasing their distinguishability.

an argument in defense of money.[5] Money could be understood as simply a tool that expresses the attribute of value for the commodity in question. However, money is not the sole path of value expression. What economic textbooks call the "double coincidence of barter"' is such a pre-money marketplace void of money where the attribute of value is verbalized through the comparison of two or more commodities. *You* are the maker of A (allow A to be goats) and want to sell your goats to acquire B (allow B to be wood). To do so someone must be willing to trade a specified number of your goats for a specified quantity of their wood. If it was agreed that you would give away one of your goats for five sheets of wood it would also establish that your goats have the value of five sheets of wood.

Money is an adolescent to the practice of trade; it was invented to simplify the act of exchange.[6] Far before the establishment of federally insured currency notes, and well before the birth of Jesus, items like coins and sea shells provided a mechanism to trade through an intermediary.[7] Such monetary devices profoundly simplify the act of trade by allowing your goats to be brought to market and exchanged for currency units.[8] What takes place in a marketplace that exchanges commodities for currency is crucial to a proper understanding of money. Commodities entering such an arena are not valuable because of there physicality or their use-values, but for what Marx calls a

---

5. The digital-generation argument could be wagered that technology, mechanized production parts, and processes of atomization allow for a widget's production without human labor input. A truth remains that all of these assistive technologies must be invented, produced and utilized by human hands. While assistive technologies allow for mass production, and less labor time on a per-unit basis, labor time is still present in the production of the primary widgets.
6. The use of the word "adolescent" is to place the practice of trade before the invention of money.
7. Graeber, 2001, *Toward.*
8. The simplification should be rudimentary from this point: money does away with the constraints of the "double coincidence of barter". With the use of money a merchant could sell his commodities for currency units and then become a consumer who could shop freely for the commodity he desired.

commodity's exchange value - the quantity of monetary units that are socially accepted as exchangeable for a given commodity.[9] Seemingly what money provides is a place to store value - value that was once in the form of a commodity - into a unit of congealed wealth that can then be later used as a metric to assess the worth of other commodities.

This conversion of value from a commodity to *a value storage unit* should not make money into a symbol of value. Quite the contrary, "...money is the value form of commodities."[10] Money is merely a form of value expression or a tool for commodities to more harmoniously express their value. For Marx however, such a device *mis-expresses* the true value of commodities. A return to your goats will elucidate this humble assertion: as you raise your goats they become a *crystallization*[11] of your labor into a useful commodity that becomes exchangeable for like value. But the market in which these goats are traded uses money - and not more goats - making money the socially necessary but categorically unfaithful partner to the exchange of an unlimited set of valuable commodities. While money cannot be anything other than symbolic, it is still essential to capital markets (and Marx's argument is in agreement with this fact). But money is not equal to

---

9. One should argue that the exchange value of a commodity is still derived from the particular commodity's useful qualities and therefore exchange values are directly linked to the commodity in question. This is a correct assertion but still in agreement with the statement made. When a sheep becomes $5 it is no long a sheep at all. Instead it is simply just 5 units of currency. Exchange values make opaque all commodities and, as will be discovered by the end of this work, make objections identical.
10. Marx, 1867, *Capital* (p.197).
11. The use of the word "crystallization" is a reference to one of Marx's more notable statements: "Use-values are primarily means of existence. These means of existence, however, are themselves products of social life, the result of expended human vital power, materialized labor. As the embodiment of social labor, all commodities are the *crystallization* of the same substance." [Marx, 1859, *Contributions* (p.122).]

value. Instead, money is a tool; it is engaged in the act of placing a numerical nomenclature over commodities.[12]

In a capital driven society, money plays the role of a value storage silo that can capture the *raw value*[13] of a commodity during exchange, and re-convert itself into a new commodity when traded. As value oscillates between the commodity and currency form, the 1859 Marxist mathematical equation "C-M-C" - a short hand for "Commodity-Money-Commodity," depicts the relationship between two different states of value. "The process of C-M-C consists of the movement C-M, the exchange of the commodity for money, or selling; [and] the opposite movement M-C, exchange of money for a commodity, or buying [...]."[14] Marx has money working as an intermediary between two commodities that would otherwise not be linked, and as a force that strengthens markets - with merchants gaining the capacity to trade commodities for raw value (or capital) and then independently choosing what new commodities to obtain.[15]

The movement of C-M-C displays the path of exchange for the purpose of consumption (or what the discipline of economics titles "simple commodity exchange"). Here money is providing an infrastructure between commodities. A capitalist's use of money is the inverse of this process where a commodity is used to gain

---

12. Marx makes a similar statement: "Money as a measure of value is the necessary form of appearance of the measure of value which is imminent in commodities, namely labour-time." [Marx, 1867, *Capital* (p.187).]

13. The term "Raw Value" will be frequently used in this work. Raw value is actual real value - much like Marx's notion of labor being the source of value for commodities.

14. Marx, 1859, *Contributions* (p. 101).

15. This contextualization of exchange forces every movement of value to be two sided. An exchange requires two parties who are each playing with the same units of value but are simultaneously conducting opposite ends of the C-M-C equation. Simply, as the consumer trades his M for C, the merchant is simultaneously trading his C for M. C-M is also always M-C; "The conversion of a commodity into money is the conversion of money into a commodity." [Marx, 1867, Capital (p.203).] An economist would add a caveat to this statement; raw value is not capital until it becomes "self-expanding," i.e., expended on the exploitation of labor.

access to more money. Money can be used to buy a commodity that can later be sold for an increased amount of money, denoted by the equation M-C-M. If you buy 1000kg of lumber on Monday for $100, and sell 1000kg of lumber on Friday for $120 you have effectively traded one silo of value for a larger silo of value at a later date. Here a commodity is being used as an intermediary between two money sets and in this way M can be made to equal M_1.[16]

An essential question at this moment of history must be asked: if one is to accept the Marxist argument that value is the output of physical human labor then how can a capitalist, who does nothing but stockpile commodities, magically increase the value of a commodity? While it remains true that labor can generate value, commodities achieve excess value through the process of marketplace valorization. This means, then, that the consumer demand for a commodity can affect the perceived value of it.[17] In turn, the work of a capitalist is one of capitalizing on the fluctuating value perceptions of commodities that a money-economy experiences.

III.

Unwavering between the consumer, the merchant, and the capitalist are the infinite connections money produces between objects. The limitation in the *double coincidence of barter* was that without an intermediary like money, commodities could only be linked together through direct exchange or merchant relationships.

---

16. This is typically regarded as "profit," where a capitalist capitalizes on fluctuations in the availability of a commodity - in this instance lumber. In a Marxist reading, the capitalist is simply manipulating, and profiting from, the value of the labor that is contained within the commodity being traded.

17. The valorization of commodities is itself a Marxist concept. He continues: "By virtue of being value, it has acquired the occult ability to add value to itself. It brings forth living offspring, or at least always lays golden eggs." [Marx, 1867, *Capital* (p.225).]

Money both produces and allows for a vast social environment with ample separation between merchants. Stated in an alternative manner, money has the capability to link together the world's objects. This benefit is also a risk, for money will only maintain these numerous connections between objects when the inhabitants of an economic system together accept a currency's ability to contain and store value. Similar to the notion of a "truth", a currency's value is only legitimized within an organized social environment.[18] The economic journalist William Greider states this notion succinctly: "Money is worthless unless everyone believes in it."[19] Because, while you may be willing to trade your goat for five tokens - thereby transferring the value of your goats into the currency tokens - your ability to retain value in these tokens for later use is governed by a social environment that must be willing to accept your tokens for their commodities.[20] Simply, social consensus around a currency is necessary for currency to function as a value container.

It is this prerequisite that Georg Simmel, a German sociologist writing at the turn of the 20th century, takes interest in. Once value silos like money have been successfully integrated into an economy, currencies become the ultimate evaluator of value. While at one stage a commodity's value could be defined by its usefulness or its innovations, money replaces this notion with a singular register of commodity assessment: this being the quantity of *money units* that can be excavated from an object. Simmel states "[Money] becomes the frightful leveler - it hollows out the core of things, their peculiarities, their specific values and their uniqueness

---

18. Ayres, *Value,* 1949.
19. Greider, 1987, *Temple* (p.226).
20. A crucial assumption, that a stable social structure is in place, is underlying this statement. It is only in such a structure, where a governing authority, laws and daily "normalcy" persists, that merchants and consumers will be able to use currency tokens. The building of such an environment is complex and will not be described in this work. However, it is important to realize that the movement of capital cannot take place in a lawless space.

and incomparability in a way which is beyond repair."[21] As a monetary device becomes the dominant mediator of value, an economy is transformed into a statement of "how much"?

The economic disposition to hollow out commodities is not void of social backlash. Communities and merchants could revolt against a given currency - working to lessen its strength as a *true* value silo within an economy. For this reason money, by design, does not stand on its own. Rather, money has historically been legitimized through a close relationship with the chemical element of gold.[22] Gold is metallic-yellow, measured in troy ounces (1 troy ounce is equivalent to 31.1 grams), and has a unique place as both a commodity and a value signifier.[23] Most importantly, gold is an overtly scarce substance. As of 2007 only 158,000 tons of gold have been excavated from the ground.[24]

In truth, the intrinsic worth of gold is a social creation, but a keen Marxist would assert that an argument over gold's true value is a misguided quarrel.[25] While all other commodities vary in quality, shape and use, gold is always itself; gold is an unchanging, limited object that quickly acquires an ideal significance due to its function.[26] In capitalist markets reliant on exchange, gold legitimizes the transfer of value from physical to symbolic form. This is where gold's intrinsic worth is derived.[27] In such a way gold

---

21. Simmel, 1903, *Metropolis*.
22. Gold's presence in capital markets also predates Jesus. Randall Wray, a contemporary economist, notes that the first gold coins were probably minted by the government of Argos, Greece around 630 BC. The history of gold, and the catacomb of valorized stories connected to it, cement gold's presence. In truth, this valorization merely aided in generating the perception that gold has intrinsic value. [Wray, 1998, *Understanding* (p.44).]
23. National Mining Association, 2008, *History*.
24. World Gold Council, 2009, *World*.
25. Marx believed that the value of gold was directly proportional to labor.
26. These notions are Marx's. I am drawn to them, but they are not mine. Marx continues. "... Gold and silver, as elementary substances, are always the same, and equal quantities of them represent, therefore, values of equal magnitude." [Marx, 1859, *Contributions* (p.209).]
27. In "Capital Volume I" Marx suggests that gold's value is derived like the value of all other commodities: by the socially necessary labor time in its production.

is not unlike its siblings in that "...every commodity is a symbol, since, as value, it is only the material shell of the human labour expended on it." [28] As consumers, merchants, and capitalists in large numbers lack the meditative capacity to engage with gold for what it is, instead of what it does, gold becomes absorbed in two dominant processes: (1) to certify the translation of capitalism's *immense accumulation of commodities* [29] into the universal language of money, and (2) to serve as the equivalency of the value stated on currency notes - the coins, the paper bills, the sea shells - in circulation. [30]

IV.

It has always been the affluent, elite, noble and privileged classes that owned gold. Whether it was Julius Caesar bringing gold back for Rome after his victorious battles (circa 60 B.C.) or the royalty of Great Britain who demanded gold as the prominent aspect of their clothing (circa 1280 A.D.), over time gold's ownership has been successfully fetishized. [31] "Why not?" Greider rhetorically asks "...these precious metals were, after all, created by God, not man." [32] This characteristic aside, gold could be idolized for its masterful performance as two distinct commodities. First as a useful, expensive, idealized commodity that consumers can purchase and display to others, and second as a "money-

---

28. Marx, 1867, *Capital* (p.185).
29. Regarded as one of Marx's most famed lines, the phrase "an immense accumulation of commodities" has been stated in most of Marx's publications. The citation will be from "Capital" by default. [Marx, 1867, *Capital* (p.125).]
30. Economists would demand a more precise version of this statement and so one will be provided: All "non commodity money" - coins and bills - are linked to (as well as a stand in for) commodity money - a substance such as gold or copper that has real and social value. There is an argument to be waged in this distinction in that any substance *could* be given *real* value: "real value" is an arbitrarily placed tag.
31. National Mining Association, 2008, *History*.
32. Greider, 1987, *Temple* (p.230).

commodity" - a monetary device used to lubricate exchange.[33] Both of gold's roles function simultaneously, but in its second role (as a money-commodity) gold, if used directly, is a restrictive device because of its limited availability. This limitation, in fact, infuses more value into gold and, simultaneously, produces a symbolic order. Gold is freed from being physically used as a trading tool because it has lesser commodities - coins and paper bills - acting as a proxy that successfully rely on gold's fetishized value.[34] While this discovery is a philosophical quandary, the conundrum for early capitalists was not whether gold could be equated with raw value, but how to safely utilize congealed value within the economy. [35]

The origins of currency are numerous, but Greider traces them to the European goldsmiths who stored and safeguarded a citizen's gold, issuing paper receipts (or more formally "a note") attesting, and directly connected to, the customer's holdings. This is what economists would later call "private banking" - where a non-governmental authority holds gold (or other forms of raw

---

33. The use of the word lubricate is a nod to David Harvey who uses this term to talk about gold. [Harvey, 2006 *Limits.*]
34. In earlier stages of history (and this work) sea shells were part of such a listing. Sea shells perform the same social function that paper bills do, but they are not linked to gold; paper money is. It is because the substance of gold is the validator of money's value that sea shells will be dropped from this listing. Marx continues, "...since gold cannot serve in that capacity [as its own symbol], it receives a symbolical, silver or copper substitute in those spheres of circulation in which it is most subject to wear and tear, namely where purchases and sales are constantly taking place in the smallest scale." [Marx, 1859, *Contributions* (p. 145).]
35. And this is also, in part, a philosophical paper. The decision to move away from these lines of thought is only temporary as Item 3 directly confronts these topics. As will become evident after a full reading of this work, it is necessary to develop and regurgitate a depth of knowledge on a topic (in this case money, neoclassical economics, and the history of economic thought) before a philosophical deconstruction can be successful. Truth be told, gold does not equal value, in fact gold is a misdirection to the space of value, but in this section of the work one is only grappling with how gold is used, not what gold truly is.

value) for use at the command of the owner.[36] It quickly becomes clear that these paper notes were almost as valuable as the gold in storage since "...whoever owned that piece of paper could go to the goldsmith and claim the gold."[37] In most cases the goldsmith would never relinquish the gold he had in storage to the owner; the paper note could continue to circulate in the economy with the same efficacy that it continued to represent the gold in storage. As this simple schema takes hold in a community, the goldsmith becomes king.[38] What modern banking contextualizes as "lending" is the ability for the goldsmith, and later the banker, to leverage his holdings (better known as a bank's "reserves") on the profitable action of lending - where the banker issues his paper notes in excess of reserves and charges a fee for the service. This over production of notes will work only when a bank's gold reserves are perceived as representative of the value stored in a bank, meaning that an excessive overproduction of notes (understood as "over lending") will produce a degradation of value in all notes circulating.[39] Such activity is termed "fractional-reserve banking" and it is based on the premise that, as long as a reasonable amount of gold is kept in storage, a bank will be able to issue paper notes in excess of its reserves because few people will ask for their gold back once it is in storage, let alone multiple clients at the same time.

Bank lending is an act of speculation; it allows individuals to supplement their own capital with outside investment to produce valuable commodities. At its most basic level lending deploys capital to generate future demand. What must be acknowledged about banking is that it further separates value from the

---

36. Melvin, 2009, *Financial*.
37. Greider, 1987, *Temple* (p.227).
38. The role of the goldsmith, in truth, transitions into the job of a banker. The use of the world "king" is used to describe the dynamics of a relationship between a money storer and the community that uses such a service.
39. It is interesting to note that a bank that issues notes in excess of its reserves is, in fact, lying about the value of its gold holdings - for if everyone were to return these notes at one time, there would be more notes than gold available.

commodities in circulation. By hoarding gold, and removing it from the act of exchange, banks replace *value* with a more symbolic element - paper money. As towns surrender their gold in the name of security and functionality, the possibility arises that these consumers and merchants could revolt once more against a currency that they believe has lost legitimacy. Quickly, formalized banking, with its capitalist practice of lending and its affection for risk, needed their currencies and business practices to be legitimized by a higher authority. In turn, the 1775 Continental Congress of the 13 American colonies established the American Treasury which was imbued with the capacity to print paper money,[40] and also the right to sell these notes to private banks for local use.[41] These *American Dollars* were still exchangeable for gold - for the ever more fetishized idea of value - but gold held in the city of Washington.[42] Under such a schema the value of currency could become detached from a local bank and simultaneously legitimated by the federal government.[43] To its credit, America did understand one key element needed in the struggle for world wide currency recognition: having a centralized government-run authority print and lend currency.[44]

By 1912, the United States of America had approximately 30,000 banks and a nationally recognized gold price of $18.92 per

---

40. Formalized private banking did not correlate with the signing of the Declaration of Independence. These value storage facilities predated this event. [US Treasury, 2006, *History.*]
41. As banks bought American paper they sold their gold reserves to the Federal government.
42. Meltzer, 2004, *History.*
43. This is the system of fiat money and it will be elaborated in the section to come.
44. The relationship between currency and gold is similar to the relationship between banks and a centralized, government owned authority that prints currency and retains reserves: banks need the Federal Reserve like paper money needs gold.

troy ounce.[45] Most of these banks were local, with only one branch location, and few cooperated with one another - leading to a mounting list of defects. The majority of banks still issued their own currency notes, banks did not typically recognize (or accept the value in) each others self produced currencies, and inconsistencies in reserves led to an alarming number of bank failures.[46]

V.

While the U.S. Treasury provided the modern template of commodity exchange, it was the Federal Reserve, chartered by the American Congress in 1913 and operational by 1914, that mandated the modern form of value circulation.[47] In 1919 Edwin Kemmerer, a notable American monetary economist, wrote a timely and positive review of the then newly established Federal Reserve (the "Fed"). What the Fed accomplished, Kemmerer explained, was not simply the unification of "... independent banks with all their essential functions, but [the federation of] them into a unified system which is democratic in its organization and

---

45. The banks that issued the dollar exclusively were easy to find. They were in New York, Chicago, Philadelphia, Boston, San Francisco and other large, growing, metropolitan centers. Also, between 1850 and 1913, the price of gold rose $.01. [The National Mining Association, 2008, *Historical.*] [Kemmerer, 1919, *ABC.*]
46. There is a conscious choice to focus on the inner-workings of "American capitalism" in this work. Karen Ho, the writer of *Liquidated*, makes a similar choice in her work after the realization that "... Capitalism in the U.S. is routinely conflated with "western capitalism" or global capitalism, understood and universal, rational and natural, and represented as the pinnacle of capitalist development..." (p.327) America has never not been the ethos of "capital-in-the-making" and in this way rendering America the subject of dissection allows for a rich conversation about money and capital that is unrestrained by social boundaries or territories. [Ho, 2009, *Liquidated.*]
47. The modern version of the Fed, nicknamed "the harmonious 12 banks", began in 1935 after several rounds of reform. This version is still operating today. [The Board of Governors of The Federal Reserve System, 2005, *Federal.*]

nationwide in its field of operation."[48] Kemmerer continued to boast of the Fed's ability to mandate monetary policy, increase the elasticity of money and consolidate the verity of notes in circulation, all while streamlining the transfer of money from one bank to the next.

What is undeniable is the Fed's immediate supremacy over a large quantity of otherwise disconnected commodities and other valuable assets.[49] But the capabilities and duties of the Fed are not simply these economic mandates. The Federal Reserve System of the United States of America was a calculated and imaginative response to a marketplace that, because of its expansion, mutated a society - making markets reliant on value that could not be seen, touched or accessed. The movement of gold from the home to the bank to a secured facility within the government elucidates this point; the idea of value sustains the circulation of commodities, not the presence or use of gold. For, at this moment in the 20th century, paper money had gained greater socially recognized value than any singular commodity ever had. A return to the Marxian revelation that money is not *truly* value also demands a reading of the American market as one that had lost the ability to distinguish between a monetary device like dollars and a valuable input like human labor - the two had become indistinguishable or even the same.

Before displaying the functionality of the Fed through Greenspan, Greider, Hazlitts, Marx, Meltzer, and company, it is important to recall what money is. Money is a socially supported value container; when capitalists and consumers store their gold or other earnings in a bank, they believe in a bank's ability to safeguard value. The trust consumers have in banks is particularly interesting because it cannot be denied that banks, at the turn of the

---

48. Kemmerer, 1919, *ABC* (p.28).
49. To insure a level of stability, the Fed did demand that all banking, lending and investment institutions work exclusively within the confines of the American dollar. [Kemmerer, 1919, *ABC*.]

20th century, feasted on the deposits of perceived raw value forms (like coper, metal, diamonds) only to issue symbolic notes. The belief in a bank's ability to safeguard value, it seems, is more honestly the belief that such symbolic forms of value are directly correlated to a bank's reserves. But just as money is a socially supported symbol of value, one must also question whether these raw elements of value are anything other than such a symbol as well. Indeed, to talk about the differences between metal and paper-based money is a conversation centered on aesthetics.[50] Metal coins were capable of expressing their value in their weight, their numerical quantity and their historic social validity. Paper, at first sight, feels and looks worthless - with only the issuer's reserves and its numerical number defending its value.[51] But both are valuable, in the end, because the larger social environment recognizes them as such.

These visual and physical distinctions are the basis of Irving Fisher's *money illusion* hypothesis - where the value stated on paper currency is perceived by the user as the same thing as real raw value contained within coins.[52] His 1929 statement was guided by the notion that paper money was a lesser version of weighted coins. In truth, paper money does have added functionality over coins. However, Fisher's money illusion hypothesis is misguided, not because it assumes a naive consumer but because gold and

---

50. Milton Friedman, who will be a central figure in Item 2, seems to favor gold and copper-based money for precisely this rationale. [Friedman,1992, *Money*.]
51. When using a weighted money-commodity (like gold), buying grains or other weight-based items relied on marking the weight of money to the weight of the commodity to be sold (such as 5 grams of wheat is equal to 1 gram of gold). Paper money has no equivalency, instead 1 gram of wheat is equal to 5 units of money.
52. Fisher, 1928, *Money*.

dollars are in fact the same economic tool.[53] Both facilitate the process of exchange and both are fully capable value silos. Mitchell Innes, who has written extensively on the history of money, defends such a notion. He argues that because any form of money first demands social consensus, weighted money is in fact an inferior monetary device.[54] Paper currency has a simple value identifier - the numerical number stated on it; weighted currency is victim to inaccurate scales, the wear and tear (and therefore lightening) of coins, and the inevitable degradation that will ensue over the transitions it is involved in.[55] The misfortune that weighted currency succumbs to stems from its transparency; simply stated, not all coins are identical in physicality or weight so they cannot be the same value.[56] Paper currency, however, is purely symbolic - its stated value sustains its worth.[57] Theoretically, then, the Fed - a body that has the authority to control the use and functionality of the American dollar - should be able to create a superior value silo.

VI.

At the turn of the 20th century, unregulated American banks created their own currencies and leveraged a risky sum of their

---

53. First, to further defend the "added functionality of paper currency," federally issued paper currency standardizes the process of exchange, nationally legitimizes markets and allows commodities to be more subjectively evaluated. Next, to further support the claim that gold and dollars are the same economic tool, the following should be remembered: gold coins are not raw value; useful commodities and the labor who made them are.
54. Innes, 2004, *Credit.*
55. The point is that a $5 note is always $5; a 5 gram coin will quickly become 4.8 grams as it wears down in one's pocket.
56. Or, said another way, one consumer could receive more of a commodity (say a grain) for his one gram coin then the a subsequent consumer depending on the variance between the two supposedly socially identical coins.
57. The argument here should be straightforward; every $10 bill has exactly the same value. Because of this there is no need to weigh or measure a desired commodity against the $10. Said another way, $10 is always $10.

reserves; the Fed needed to quickly ensure a bank's reserves from defaulting on American consumers, who, in the event of a bank failing, could lose their savings. For this reason, the Fed was envisioned to be a banker's bank - a body that would validate and regulate banks by providing emergency access to additional money, even when a bank did not have the reserves to pay for such notes. Greider formalizes this position, stating that: "the Federal Reserve system [operates] like the modern equivalent of the king's keep - a separate storehouse alongside the private economy and independent of its force."[58] With this reading the Fed was built to be the rudder of an unruly economy. The capabilities of this institution are best understood, not through the Fed's stated processes, but through the visual event of a bank failure. For it is when a bank fails that one can truly witness the power American dollars have over the minds of consumers and the power the Fed has over money.

Banks fail when they physically run out of currency. The risk that the goldsmith took when he loaned merchants his notes in excess of his gold reserves is a precursor to a bank that has leveraged its reserves to the point where it can no longer honor note holders that wish to collect on their contractual holdings.[59] This event has been identified as a seasonal, location specific, bank failure because such an event would typically occur during the harvesting months when farmers needed lines of credit - cash - to bring their produce to market. Inevitably, the bank in distress would be low on either its own paper notes or American dollars, without an emergency supply of money.

---

58. Greider, 1987, *Temple* (p.32).
59. The conflict is that banks have a disposition to lend because this action is a source of profit. However, bank lending has a positive correlation with the dilution of bank reserves because when banks lend their gold reserves do not increase, but their payment obligations do. In turn, each troy ounce of gold must be leveraged against a larger sum of paper in circulation. While the ideal lending scenario is one where banks receive their paper back with interest, not all lending is profitable. Simply, aggressive lending correlates with a high risk of loss. [Melvin, 2009, Financial.]

The scene outside the First National Bank of Ogden, Utah in 1931 was typical of such an impending failure, with long lines of nervous depositors who had heard the speculation traveling throughout the town of a reserve shortage and were hoping to be lucky enough to make it to the teller window before the bank ran out of currency notes. Greider tells the story of Marriner Eccles, president of First National, who told his tellers "The best we can do is slow it down. People are going to come here to close out their savings accounts. You are going to pay them. But you are going to pay them very slowly. It's the only chance we have to deal with the panic."[60] The meandering by the tellers merely heightened the tension; thankfully Eccles had put in a call to the Federal Reserve branch of Salt Lake City that dispatched an emergency caravan of fresh American dollars that reached his bank just before his bank's 3 p.m. closing. Once the armed Federal Reserve guards had entered the bank, Eccles emerged from behind the bank tellers' windows to address the crowd:

"Many of you have been in line for a considerable time. I notice a lot of pushing and shoving and irritation. I just wanted to tell you that instead of closing at the usual hour of three o'clock, we have decided to stay open just as long as there is anyone who desires to withdraw his deposits or make one. Therefore, you people who have just come in can return later this afternoon or in the evening if you wish. There is no justification for excitement or the apparent panicky attitude on the part of some depositors. As all of you have seen, we have just had brought up from Salt Lake City a large amount of currency that will take care of all your requirements. There is plenty more where that came from."[61]

---

60. Greider, 1987, *Temple* (p. 304).
61. Greider, 1987, *Temple* (p.305).

The Fed has an unlimited amount of American dollars.[62] Unlike a bank that is bound to the confines of deposits and reserves, the Federal Reserve can literally create and destroy value silos with a decree. While these powers can be recognized as unsound, it is the Fed that saved The First National Bank of Ogden and not Eccles's speech. All the patrons needed was assurance that their savings were safe; all they needed was the visual presence of the Federal Reserve to disperse calmly from the bank lobby. Even the customers who closed out their accounts opened new ones to redeposit their money. Regardless of the Fed's powers, bank panics are, above all else, a human event. For Charles Calomiris and Gary Gorton, two economists who have intensely studied the banking industry, economic panics are the emotional result of consumers who (for a variety of reasons and rumors) become uncertain of a bank's health.[63] The result is an *asymmetric effect* - when one consumer's perceived risk drives many to withdraw their money. As risk runs through a community the human emotion of fear is the source that generates an impending bankruptcy and not a fluctuation in a bank's reserves. Inversely, money's value is sustained when confidence and reliance in an economy's money supply is prevalent.

Any currency a bank can issue is a symbol of value, and nothing more. If money is to sustain its value it is because of the social confidence that has been built around it - where an economy has an allegiance to a symbol, like paper currency. For such a

---

62. For some, the technical process of self generated federal currency may be interesting: When the Fed needs money, it engages in a merry-go-round (and purely accounting book) process with the Department of the Treasury. The Fed buys American dollars at face value from the Treasury; the Treasury records a debit on its balance sheet and the Fed enters a credit on its balance sheet. The Fed can then loan out these funds to the "party in need" at favorable terms. When the distressed party repays the Fed, the Fed sends the profit into the Federal budget and simultaneously gives the loan amount back to the Treasury. The transaction, on paper, looks like it never took place. Some elements of this analysis come from Friedman. [Friedman, 1992, *Money*.]

63. Calomiris, 2000, *Origins*.

relationship to be everlasting, "[o]ne thing is necessary, [Marx asserts] the symbol of money must have its own objective social validity." [64] Written in 1867, Marx is forecasting the American dollar; he is asserting that paper currencies can function as the symbolic form of universal value but not without a socially recognized connection back to defendable objective value.[65] The claim that money cannot function without social relevance is a warning to the power money has if left unchecked; if a citizen of a monetary economy is unable to locate the origin of a currency's value, the argument follows that money has effectively covered up or dislocated itself from the root of value. In theory the Federal Reserve was constructed to guard against this risk by strengthening the connection between currency - a symbol - and the notion of raw value. The question becomes how effective the Federal Reserve has been at managing such a risk and sustaining such a relationship. What the Fed must keep alive is an orthodoxy of epic proportions - that the paper currency it issues to banks and consumers is not just a symbol of value but an element of value.

64. Marx, 1867, *Capital* (p.226).

65. For Marx the category of objective value would be labor.

Item 2: Money's Worth

Randall Wray would be unsatisfied with the narrative choices made in the prior Section. For while at this juncture a set of relationships has been firmly established - raw value can be found in the productive human; gold is a symbol for this raw value; dollars are a symbol for gold; the Fed is the sole manufacturer of dollars; currency is nothing but a tool that greases the action of exchange - Professor Wray is a firm believer that money is "... not meant to provide a medium of exchange, but rather [is] evidence of the state's debt... [.] ...Coins [are] then nothing more than 'tallies' - evidence of government debt... [.]"[1] If this University of Missouri-Kansas Professor is correct to dismiss the notion that money is the child of an antiquated system of barter, accreting instead that

---

[1]. Wray, 1998, *Understanding* (p.46).

currency is simply a tool invoked by the "state [or the sovereign] to impose a tax-debt on its subjects... [,]"[2] then Dr. Friedman's opening chapter in his book Money Mischief, *The Island of Stone Money*, is the discovery of money's true origin.

In Friedman's opening chapter he invokes the Caroline Islands, a land purchased by the German government in 1898 from Spain, where formalized currencies were not in use. Such a non-monetary economy presented a problem to the Germans, who needed to modernize the island's roads and walkways and wanted to pay (with government backed currency) the natives to perform such manual labor. However, because the native *Failu* had no understanding of money, offering them German coins in exchange for their labor would be little motivation to perform these repairs. Instead, the German government sent a messenger to each of the townships. These government employees marked buildings and homes with black crosses denoting that these spaces were to be government property until the manual labor was completed.

> *"This instantly worked like a charm; the people, being dolefully impoverished, turned to and repaired the highways to such a good effect from one end of the island to the other, that they are now like park drives. Then the government dispatched its agents and erased the crosses. Presto! The fine was paid, the happy Failu's resumed possession of their [dwellings]."[3]*

The Germans were not lucky; instead they understood that money is the physical representation of power and that such a force can be reproduced in various ways. And when painted black crosses can provide the same function as paper money, the textbook invention of the *double coincidence of barter* dissolves.

---

2. Ibid.
3. Friedman, 1994, *Money* (p 5).

Instead, as Wray's work undeniably finds, money is nothing more than "the purposeful intervention of government rather than [a] 'common consent' of our bartering forebears."[4] With conviction, then, there can be no such thing as currency without the presence of societal leaders - such figures create and sustain the demand for money as they levy taxes and provide services that can only be *paid* for with these government issued notes.[5] But, the conception of money as a form of sovereign control does not disavow the first finding, which is that that money is meant to symbolize value.[6]

However, money needs an operator, a controller, a manager, an endorsor and an enforcer. Dollars do not naturally exist, they are instead produced *on fiat* by a specific entity; for this reason money always has a creator. In America, the Federal Reserve, and more generally the United States government, is this authority figure. Before the Fed, other managers provided much of the same function - these were the local banks, and before them the town goldsmith and the king.[7] This notion, that all money is the sovereign's creation and under his ownership, is also the conceptual framework of *fiat money* - classically defined as currency notes, issued, backed and created by the federal

---

4. Wray, 1998, Understanding (p.53).
5. Monetary policy will be discussed shortly and this statement requires this further reading. It is important to grasp at this moment that there can only be as much money in circulation as the government allows. Money neither grows on trees, nor is it "created" by the market. Instead a fixed quantity of currency oscillates inside of a market, from one person and corporation to the next. The government - the Fed - can expand the money supply as it issues loans and creates more services, effectively creating a larger demand for money.
6. The reason, therefore, for using paper bills instead of a tallying system like the one used on the Caroline Islands is purely one of convenience. Society could agree to keep track of wealth by making markings on houses - it's simply that walking around with dollar bills that signify the possession of value is much less cumbersome.
7. In fact, almost all of today's governments (even those operating within so called third world territories) have a federal reserve type agency that is the issuer and operator of a currency. To reiterate from earlier footnotes, the United States of America is the focus of this paper only because it is the de facto symbol of capital's operation.

government and declared as legal tender, irredeemable for any other type of note.[8] Fiat money (from this point the equivalent of American issued paper) is meant to retain what Marx defined as the function of money: "to serve as the form of appearance of the value of commodities."[9] But, while Marx would trace gold coins and all other money forms back to the underlying value in a commodity (that being labor), the underlying value of fiat money is the ruler that issued it.[10] While not expressed or commonly identified, fiat money is given to the laborer in exchange for his work, it is not produced by him.

Marx's 19th and 20th century version of money is constrained by the relative inelasticity of that period's currency - gold - as the volume of gold that can circulate in an economy is limited to the physical amount of gold that can be minted for that

8. A consolidated view of history is contained in this statement. America has a long history of setting a price (trending upwards over time) at which the dollar can be exchanged for a set amount of gold. The Breton Woods Agreement was ratified in December of 1945 by the United States of America and all major European and Asian nations, and established a globally fixed conversion rate of $35 USD to one ounce of gold. This effectively made the American dollar both the reserve currency of all western nations and established a close relationship between the value of gold and the value of the dollar. This also meant that nations no longer had to hold a fixed amount of gold, because they knew that the value of the dollar always had a fixed (non-fluctuating) conversion rate to gold. It was the Nixon administration that terminated this gold to dollar convertibility in August of 1971. The effect of this action was the removal of an underlying commodity (gold) to support the U.S. dollar - allowing both to be freely valued within the global marketplace. [Meltzer, 2004, *History*] [Greider, 1987, *Secrets*] [Friedman, 1963, Monetary]

9. Marx, 1867, *Capital* (p.184).

10. This sentence is constructed with precision; one could ask if a ruler (governor, government, issuer) truly embodies and stands in for the value of fiat currency or if they merely manage it. This work sides with the former stance. For without the sovereign fiat money would not exist. Further, the claim made to fiat money's value is that these notes are "legal tender for all debts, public and private, and... redeemable in lawful money at the United State Treasury or any Federal Reserve Bank". These words, imprinted on every American dollar, place the value of these notes squarely on the Fed and the sovereign itself. The ruler imbues fiat money with its value, with its status as legal tender, with its redeem-ability for *lawful money* - a term that could mean nothing else but what we have, in this analysis, been calling raw value.

market. Fiat money has no such constraint, it is "elastic".[11]   If the state wishes to expand the volume of money circulating in an economy, it can simply print more currency - placing it within the expanding market sectors of its choosing. This truth must have weighed on Franklin Delano Roosevelt, in 1933, during the depths of the Great Depression as he contemplated the monetary policy that would bring the country back to prosperity. Laborers and capitalists were in need of money and new venues to obtain it; the gold that was still in free circulation was far too valuable and sparse to be socially useful. So, that year Roosevelt suspended the active exchange of gold for dollars, seized all gold coins, and began to rapidly print dollars that would be available through public works projects.[12] In essence, Roosevelt was minting dollars with a decree. Still the importance of this event is not that Roosevelt's policy "worked", but that American citizens, even in the most desperate of circumstances, still wanted to be paid with dollars - and not a slew of other raw valuable goods. In this instance America retained and even strengthened its belief in the dollar as the mechanism to prosperity.

---

11. Elasticity is used here to contrast the limited availability of a physical monetary currency, such as gold, with a fiat based currency that can grow or contract at the will of the sovereign.

12. The hard economic (or mathematical) sections of this conversation are intentionally being placed in footnotes because of a belief that such dialogue is dry and, in large part, a regurgitation of many academic works. Even so I will continue with the inner-workings of Roosevelt's policy. The Roosevelt Administration was able to print new money because it increased, on fiat, the ratio between the required amount of gold that needed to be on hand at the U.S. Treasury and the quantity of dollars in circulation - making each ounce of gold worth more dollars. But the Fed also liberalized its balance sheet, allowing it to balloon to an unprecedented sum. Most economists, including current Chairman of the Federal Reserve Ben Bernanke, have posited that the true mistake of the Great Depression was that these liberal policies were not applied soon enough or for a long enough duration. [Greider, 1987, *Secrets*] [Friedman, 1963, *Monetary*] [The National Mining Association, 2008, *Historical*.]

II.

This belief in the American Dollar is beyond the discipline of economics and also beyond writers who are confined by this discipline's line of logic. For what is special about dollars is their pure symbolic worth. This perception, that dollars are the ultimate value container, is not the work of the sovereign; these notions come from an external place - from a social thesis around money that stipulates that dollars will be forever valuable.[13] And for capital markets (where fiat money is used with pride) such an ethos is always grounded around the two sided *Keynesian* coin of uncertainty and confidence. John Maynard Keynes was not just a 20th century British born economist, he is also the monetary thinker who discovered the boundaries of currency and its speculative mechanism of value creation.

The most appropriate way to grapple with Keynes is through rejection. Orthodox, classical, laissez-faire, theories of monetary-based economies often rely on self governing, invisible, and powerful "market forces" to create more value, profit and prosperity. This dominant paradigm, championed by Milton Friedman and Adam Smith, allows a complex topic like money to be unjustly simplified because it stipulates that everything - currency, people, and commodities - on a macro scale, are harmoniously operating for the betterment of the market itself.[14]

---

13. This statement should be read with a clear distinction between the notion of "perception" and "creation". The government - the sovereign - will always be the creator of money, but the perception of money as the ultimate commodity is a human feeling. This notion will be further explained in the text.
14. The evidence of this in Friedman's, Smith's and many other monetarists is nothing short of pervasive. Friedman's 1974 claim that "a change in the price of any good can always be attributed to a change in either demand or supply"; Smith's 1776 notion of an *invisible hand* that moves all market forces in a common direction; Jean-Baptiste Say's 1767 work around the ability for a producer's production of goods to self create demand, all point directly to a market that can work harmoniously. The principal argument of this work is that such notions are misplaced and misguided.

Keynes responds: "[i]t may well be that the classical theory represents the way in which we should like our economy to behave. But to assume that it actually does so is to assume our difficulties away."[15] His 1936 work, "The General Theory", provides an opening for money's validity as a transparent valuable tool to be brutally questioned because, as Keynes states, "a monetary economy ... is essentially one in which changing views about the future are capable of influencing... its direction."[16] Keynes forces us to see that money's value is backed by a blind agreement of market forces that think an "...existing state of affairs will continue indefinitely."[17]

Where this discussion leads is the melding together of the market at large and its various social actors. Both are victims of having a complicit confidence in what can be nothing more than the malleable paper commodity of fiat money. What is so alarmingly precarious about money, then, is that this device is not just a symbol of value. It is also a speculative device, a way to place a wager on the future because the impending perception of money will affect its societal worth.[18] That is, a Keynesian view of money frees currency from its static value, attaches the device to the dynamic space of *the market*, and allows its worth to directly

---

15. Keynes, 1936, *General* (p.34).
16. *Ibid.* vii
17. Keynes could have been been introduced into this writing at various points. He could have been used in the beginning lines when talking about Capitalville as a figure that complicates Friedman's working simulation, or as a thinker that understood the true emotions of The First National Bank customers as they saw the Federal Reserve truck pull up. The goal is not to use Keynes as a filibuster against classical economists but as a deeper, theoretical thinker. He is searching for the "value of money" - a topic that this paper has only started to directly grapple with.
18. The post Keynesian work of Professor Hyman Philip Minsky provides more color to this statement: "What is essential, even fundamental to any interpretation of Keynes is to recognize that Keynes came to the problems of economic choice that involve time (and thus uncertainty), and the behavior of an economy in which such choices are important." [Minsky, 1975, *John* (p.65).]

fluctuate with the human emotion of confidence.[19] Fiat money was never worth the specific commodity it was being exchanged for; its value has always been guided by the abstract idea of *the market* - an accumulation of forces that all share in common their use of paper money.

At this juncture, one can only posit that the value of money is at best speculative because it rides on the back of human emotions. As Keynes described it, "[m]admen in authority, who hear voices in the air..."[20] are blindly using a monetary device to evaluate value. Nevertheless, Friedman is still correct to assert that "...money is whatever is generally accepted in exchange for goods and services."[21] Most place the writings of Keynes and Friedman on opposing ends of economic theory. While it is evident that these thinkers contextualize money differently - Friedman holds fast to the notion that money is a grounded asset, in use by the market and under the market's control, while Keynes' view is one of instability and human psychology - Keynes and Friedman are not directly in conversation with each other.[22] Friedman's work maps the internalities of markets (how market forces[23] work, function, and grow); the Keynesian project is one of discovery, one that allows the cryptic object of money to be opened.

---

19. Keynesianism, then, recognizes the inherently social, dynamic and fictitious character of money.
20. Keynes, 1936, *General* (p.383).
21. Friedman, 1994, *Money* (p.16).
22. Worse, because Friedman holds his monetary theories to the notion that resources are always optimally employed, money is simply (and obtusely) greasing the wheels of exchange with no independently derived worth.
23. The use of *market forces* should itself be questioned. It is a *Smithian* (Adam Smith) term packed with unjust simplification. The "market" is made up of an immense accumulation of diverse commodities and not a select few "market forces." Such terms are responsible for many misguided views on money, and should be rejected. The term will be used in this work for the last time.

III.

Confidence is what determines money's worth; *uncertainty* is what can degrade the value of the dollar. When pundits, investors, politicians and laborers are confident in the future of the dollar, the worth of this device rises.[24] When we are uncertain or fearful of our economy, the value of the dollar fails to live up to its expectations. But this conversation can quickly become vague if not grounded in an investigation of money as it moves within an economy. So, like the consumers who find their pockets empty, the instinct to return to an examination of banking institutions is necessary.

Based on Federal Reserve audits, America's 50 largest banks privately manage $14.2 trillion of these speculative currency notes.[25] The business model for these firms is still much the same as the goldsmith's - leverage deposits to issue loans - but with large scale consolidation.[26] Unlike previous periods, when thousands of local banks made loans, now only a handful of institutions are responsible for virtually all underwriting.[27] The profit of this model is the potential return on capital[28] that banks can earn, but this requires a confidence in the future - a confidence in a borrower's

---

24. The value of the dollar will rise in comparison to other currencies and in the minds of those who use it.

25. That number in long form looks like this: $14,211,295,912,000. The 10 largest banks manage about 75% of this number. [Federal Reserve System, *National Information Center: Top 50 Bank Holding Companies*, January 2010]

26. Hyman Minsky would argue that It would be misguided to assume that a bank's lending activities are its primary task. Instead "the fundamental banking activity is accepting, that is, guaranteeing that some party is creditworthy." It is for this reason that government and banks have such a close relationship - both are in the business of building confidence. [Minsky, 2008, *Stabilizing* (p.256)]

27. Loan underwriting is a financial term that means the amount of money that is being issued to the borrower.

28. The term "return on capital" means the profit earned on the money committed to a specific activity. If a capitalist were to give a home buyer a $100,000 loan and get 4% interest over 30 years, then the capitalist will get $231,746 (the *return on capital* amount) over the $100,000 issued.

ability to repay. Again, this industry has continuously shown an inability to self regulate, to remain immune from volatility, to show long term durability, and for these reasons the sovereign is intimately involved in the banking industry.[29]

The argument is that the Federal government is essential to banking because in fact banks cannot operate by themselves. Every day these risk-taking institutions use "short term capital" - money that is active in the financial system for only days at a time - that the Fed issues to them. Because the sovereign can create and destroy money, providing money to banks is only as difficult as the decision to do so. The question is why has short term currency become essential for banking institutions.[30]

Banks, who have always made loans before they have the reserve capital to back them, would become increasingly leveraged if they could not find additional reserves. In the pre-Fed era, where banks who over loaned became insolvent and failed, banking was restrained for fear of over lending against reserves.[31] With federal short term currency, such a fear is lessened because banks use the Fed as a backstop against their increased loan to reserve ratio. For Greider two options arise to keep banks solvent even as they increase their lending: "The banks could borrow the needed reserve found in the money market [this would be the expensive option] or, if excess reserves were scarce, the banks would be compelled to turn to the discount window at the Fed and get the funds there... [this would be the preferred option]."[32] The discount window is a

---

29. The sovereign is intimately involved for another reason: banks are playing with its product. The sovereign has an inherent interest in making sure its only paper is being properly cared for, thereby sustaining the demand for its fiat currency.
30. Refer to Item 1, part IV, for historic banking practices.
31. In other words, before the Fed, a bank either needed to wait for outstanding loans to be repaid or find new wealthy depositors whose savings could be used as a way to lower the bank's loan to reserve ratio.
32. Greider, 1987, *Secrets* (p.208).

term of art - equivalent to the parent that never says no.[33] It is the preferred method of short term capital because the interest rate (in this case referred to as the "discount rate") at which this Federal money is issued is not frequently altered and because any bank that asks for money is guaranteed to get it.[34] Greider continues: "If the Fed refused on any given day to supply the reserves the banking system needed, then the scramble for scarce resources would become desperate and inevitably some banks would come up short - that is, perhaps fail."[35]

What is chilling about this relationship between private industry and government is not the cooperation between them, but the message such an alliance and co-dependence brings. This intimacy, meant to securitize the nation's savings and eagerly called for by bankers who wanted to lessen the risk of defaulting on what was becoming the sum of the nation's wealth, has left the Fed boxed in to helping an industry that has always made profit through

---

33. Before the 1929 stock market crash the discount window was a booth at the New York stock exchange manned by federal employes. If a bank wanted/ needed more money for its business activities, bank representatives could walk up to the window and arrange for the cash to be transferred. Today, the discount window has been replaced by a digital representation on a computer screen, which is accessible to all member banks through the click of a mouse. Later, in Item 3, a discussion on the digitization of money will take place.

34. The discount window is also a quick way to determine the spread - the separation between the cost of capital and the return on capital. If the Fed's discount rate is at 2% and a bank is making loans at 4.5%, then the spread is 2.5%. When banks raise capital from other sources the discount rate is a negotiable number, often with a shorter spread because private lenders demand a higher return on capital. The discount window is not operated by the government as a way to make money (although it could be). Instead, the discount rate is used as a federal lever that can change the base cost of money. This lever will be talked about in greater detail shortly. To provide more information on how the discount window operates, the following should also be taken into consideration: banks do not keep this Federal money for long periods. Instead they give the money back as they get new deposits and as older loans are repaid. To limit misuse, if a particular bank is seen as overusing the window, the Fed will launch a regulatory investigation. Also, banks are "guaranteed to get" the extra money they need because a bank failure would cause a social panic around the safety of money as a value storage device, It is in the interest of the sovereign to eliminate this risk.

35. Greider, 1987, *Secrets* (p.209).

risk. Even more, the Fed must continue to provide short term capital to banks because not doing so signals a lack of confidence in the economy itself; and banks cannot operate without federal assistance, without being cared for and protected by their parents.[36]

It should come as little surprise then that it is the loaning function of a bank that can make a bank insolvent. Loaning is a speculative act because it requires a gamble on the borrower's ability to both repay the loan and to turn a profit. As is true with all bets, not all of them pan out; losses are an assumed byproduct of loaning. But if confidence is to be sustained (and the worth of money along with it) then banks must find ways to highlight gambles that are profitable while hiding ones that failed. The solution is found in "risk" - with more risk providing the potential of bets giving out greater rewards. But, if money is the device that is being loaned, then money is also the device that has become the centerpiece of such speculative bets on the future and, arguably, is worth only the proposed future prosperity banks will bring.

Banks utilize money according to Marx's M-C-M equation - utilizing money to gain access to more money instead of a diverse choice of commodities. To accomplish this banks must convert money into a commodity that can later be converted back to a larger quantity of money.[37] Loans are a way to run money through an M-C-M equation, taking the place of the commodity that should increase in value over time. Such bets on the future are speculative because they rely on the premise that money stored in a commodity form will yield more money at a later date. However, bank reserves (and private capital) can be used for numerous types of bets on the future that all obey Marx's inverted equation and all use the Fed as a backstop for their imputed risk. These speculative bets unfold in the New York stock market, a place where the world's capital comes to parlay accumulated bank notes on tomorrow's news. This is an overtly Keynesian behavior, as such activity is powered by emotions and beliefs.

---

36. As all parents do, the Fed creates rules, regulations and restrictions of acceptable activities.
37. For more on this practice see Item 1, part II.

A space like the stock market complicates the Marxian relationship between labor and consumer, because in this space money is generating more money without the direct sale or acquisition of commodities.[38] Keynes understands this disjointed relationship when he states: "[in the stock market it] ... is as though a farmer, having tapped his barometer after breakfast, could decide to remove his capital from the farming business between 10 and 11 in the morning and reconsider whether he should return to it later in the week."[39] Placing money in the stock market vastly increases the speed of value appreciation because it obscures the world of the physical.

Instead, what remains is an implied confidence that all the laborious tasks that produce value are in fact taking place, even if not seen. But in a space that has come to exchange the net sum of an economy's value, money is unhooked from the commodity and is constantly made more volatile as it moves from one bet to the next. More importantly, such an arena is competitive because winning is gauged by who is most capable of forecasting the future outcome of bets made. These are Keynes' *animal spirits* - an overwhelming emotional disposition to incorrectly value market assets based on a biased vision of the future. And, Keynes adds, "[w]hen the capital development of a country becomes a by-product of the activities of a casino, the job is likely to be ill-done."[40] The stock market is an ambiguous space, an idealized version of marketplace activity where the underling buying and selling of commodities is assumed and where all that is being bet on is how successful merchants will be.

The implied function of money is not one of speculation, it is one of evaluation. As money traverses through these speculative markets it is being used as a tool, as a way to value not the commodities of today but the commodities and economies of the future. This activity could be considered Marxian in that a stock market uses dollars as a comparative tool - as a way to assess value

---

38. Marx would claim that such a space consists of fictitious capital - this will be grappled with in Item 3.

39. Keynes, 1936, *General* (p.151).

40. *Ibid.* p.159.

for the underlying commodities that are being traded. But the actors in such a space are not concerned with value assessment. Instead, capitalists are concerned with profit retention. For them money is a tool for creating, and not identifying or labeling, value.

IV.

A controversy is afoot. Money, at best, is worth less than the tangible commodities in a market but its value is accepted by the market as transient - fluctuating with the human trait of confidence. If Marx's worries are manifesting themselves, if people are unable to trace the value in currency back to an underlying commodity[41] but only to abstract notions like the sovereign, the bank, the market or more money, then the currency traveling through capital markets is of purely imaginary worth. And even if neoclassical economic theorists base market stability on grounded principles like "the internal dynamics of business that are self correcting," "supply and demand," "the perpetual growth of new industry" and, "the propensity to trade", this ground is supported by nothing but a belief in an internal functionality - internal in that even the best economic graphs, business plans, and financial models are worthless without a blinding confidence in the value of the dollar.[42] For Hyman Minsky, those who are faithful to these assumptions have downed goggles of confidence: "in our world of imperfect knowledge and imprecise actions, standard theoretical analysis posits either perfect knowledge or a fantastic capacity to compute."[43] But monetary economies, where companies and governments make multi-year forecasts on earnings, are supported by an ideological system of knowledge that consistently believes it can posit a perfect view of the future. These visions of the future

---

41. More precisely to a laborer who has produced a commodity.
42. A key claim is being made in this statement that should be further explained; these neoclassical economic concepts are able to sustain a *ground* - a fundamental outlook and belief structure - only when subjects en-mass accept these concepts as gospel.
43. Minsky, 2008, *Stabilizing* (p.116).

are built with money, calculated with money, and valued with money.

The problem, then, is that we misuse money or believe that money is capable of completing actions that in reality it can not. Still, economies use money as if it were an all purpose barometer and such abuse is the site of the imperfections and incorrect predictions that consistently arise in monetary economies. But these imperfections cannot be spoken of with such terminology by economists. Instead, these imperfections are spoken of in terms of inflation.[44] Inflation is the rate at which a currency loses value or becomes less valuable when compared to other commodities.[45] And, while the rate of inflation has varied wildly over time, it is a constant, meaning that the value contained in each unit of currency is continuously weakening. Inflation happens when monetary bets on the future exceed the net value of productive output in an economy;[46] such an excess is the result of economic actors who have misused money by placing bets on the future. This is an abstract concept that means little without an example - luckily financing a war is a prime example of inflationary behavior.

The financing of a war often requires funds that are in excess to that available for basic government operations which have been levied through tax revenue. Quite literally then, when America enters a war it needs to print money to pay for the personnel, tools, and transportation costs associated with such an

---

44. It should come as no surprise, however, that for neoclassical economists inflation is always the result of an error on the part of the government. For them inflation arises when the quantity of currency notes within the economy increases at a faster rate than the amount of money currently being used to purchase commodities - the larger the discrepancies, the larger the rate of inflation. Because the government is a printing press, the argument goes, rulers can finance their operations with this *extra* or new money. [Friedman, *Monetary*, 1963] The problem with this view is that private industry can take out loans and finance future spending with much the same ease, functionality and consequence.

45. The classic example of this is the shifting expenses of goods over time. If an apple costs $1 today and about $1.15 next year, this extra 15 cents is the accrued inflation.

46. Their are several events that can directly cause inflation. The argument here is not this endless list but what inflation, at its root, is.

endeavor. Regardless of the short term ability to borrow these funds from individual investors or nations, the monetary cost of war is only as real as the future revenue that can be collected to pay for it.[47] In a scenario that has transpired many times before in American history, a government's ability to have an unbalanced checking account - where spending is in excess of revenue - allows use of money that has yet to be taxed and reclaimed by the government. Because society retains confidence in the future, and the ability to pay for expenditures at some later date, excess spending does not result in a market's immediate demise, rather this behavior creates inflation.[48] A neoclassical economist would not refute such a claim; when there is an increase in the volume of dollars for an arbitrary reason - when more dollars are printed without a direct increase in the productive output of a society - the result is inflation, where more dollars are accounting for the same amount of value (or the same number of commodities) and with each monetary unit now accounting for less value. War produces this exact effect because such an undertaking places money into a lottery where there is a large expenditure that can only be paid for

---

47. Borrowing money should be viewed as the non-optimal measure because this action creates a compounded revenue problem. Funding will need to be found for both the borrowed sum and the interest (a fee for the privilege to borrow) on the money borrowed. The optimal maneuver would be to spend only existing revenue.

48. An examination of the U.S. Civil War is useful. Estimates put the financial expenditure of Abraham Lincoln's civil war at $4 billion. After the confederate's defeat in 1865, four years of war time tax revenue had covered only 21% of costs. This discrepancy between costs and revenue is a direct cause of the 74% spike in inflation and a doubling in the social inflation rate (more commonly felt as the rise in commodity prices). While the confederate economic system collapsed, the American dollar was strengthened by a society that recognized its currency's longevity. As a result, the 79% of unfunded war costs could be repaid with ease over time. For some, adjusting these numbers for current inflation may be both valuable and interesting: a $4 billion expense in 1865 is the same as a $556.3 billion expense in 2008, equivalent to spending $139 billion a year today. To compare this to a topical event, the Federal Congressional Budget Office projects that the nine year (2001-2010) "War on Terrorism" will top $1.17 trillion, or an average yearly expense of $130 billion. [Lerner, 1954, *Monetary.*] [Potter, 1976, *Impending.*] [United States Congressional Budget Office, 2007.]

with a future unrealized gain of winning. In turn war uses dollars to place a bet on winning.[49]

Place this past reference in the context of a continuous state of inflation, one where banks and capital markets can degrade the dollars they claim to care for so much when they use it irresponsibly. Bank lending, giving consumers lines of credit and funding stock trading operations are all ways to turn a profit, but they require the same use of excess forms of money, borrowed from the Fed at a nationally set rate of interest. The Federal interest rate is the charge the sovereign places on using its currency for speculative actions. When the interest rate is low "money is cheap", speculation is encouraged and the Fed is attempting to stimulate (grow and fund) the economy. But the Fed must constantly balance this easy money policy[50] with higher interest rates - where the Fed wants to curtail inflation, and excessive speculation, but risks leaving the nation with more modest rates of growth.[51] While the Fed controls the interest rate lever, it does so in response to the market and not in anticipation of it. And because a capitalist version of success is not simply accruing money but continuously increasing the velocity of accrual, the Fed uses the

---

49. Keynes speaks to this at great length in Chapter 16 (Observation on Nature of Capital) in his magnum opus "The General Theory" when he says "value is intrinsically tied to scarcity." This is an appropriate place to talk about Keynes' Marxian loyalties, for he says in this chapter that "I sympathize, therefore, with the pre-classical doctrine that everything is produced by labour, aided by what used to be called art and is now called technique, by natural resources which are free or cost a rent [price] according to their scarcity or abundance, and by the results of past labour, embodied in assets, which also command a price according to their scarcity or abundance." [Keynes, 1936, *General* (p.213).]

50. The term "easy money" means money that can be bowered from the Federal government at a cheap interest rate - so much so that it becomes advantageous to over borrow.

51. A rapid change from a low interest rate to a high one is sure to produce negative growth for a short period of time. This is perhaps why markets like interest rates to remain constant. In addition, it is also relevant that the interest rate is set by the Federal Reserve open market committee. Inflation's formal (or text book) definition is the rate at which borrowed Federal money will accrue yearly interest if not paid back. [Harvey, 2006, *Limits*.] [Greider, 1987, *Secrets*.]

interest rate lever to either constrain the market after it has expanded or to encourage the market after it has stalled.

In sum, the controversy around money is man made. It would be easy to point to the Fed as the actor playing a game with money but it is in fact playing a reactionary game with a market that is always unsure, and always reevaluating, what money is in fact worth. If so, then currencies are not a tool provided to the masses but a way for capitalists and the sovereign to abstract from the market its value and place speculative bets on its future. Such an apparatus rewards speculation while using laborers and consumers as a pawn; and for Jean and John Comaroff this is the goal: "Neoliberalism aspires, in its ideology and practice, to intensify the abstraction inherent in capitalism itself: to separate labor power from its human context, to replace society with the market, to build a universe out of aggregated transactions."[52]

If the inflation rate displays the health of the market, its landscape must be viewed with a particular lens. Because if money is just being used to trade forms of speculation, then all speculation produces is a rate of inflation, or the rate of degradation of the physical worth of money in circulation. David Harvey, a modern English social theorist, would reinsert Marx into this conversation, and reference the Marxist principle of a physical (as opposed to a speculative) monetary market. Harvey states in his *Limits to Capital*, "[Marx] insists that money expresses a contingent social power, ultimately dependent upon the creation of real value through the embodiment of social labour in material commodities."[53] Harvey's discussion frames speculation as the enemy of a reliable, stable and honest currency. For when money becomes embroiled in the work of economic speculation - where money is conceptualized as valuable in and of itself or when "money can produce more money" without a connection to the physical world - then money becomes disconnected from the notion of value. Said another way, when the collective force of a

52. Comaroff, 2000, *Millennial* (p.305).
53. Harvey, 2006, *Limits* (p.241).

market[54] forgets the truth of a currency - that money creates nothing, but only defines the items already present - the social worth of this device not only becomes disconnected from value but unrelated to it; money becomes an illusion - a mirage, a trace, - of value that exists only in the *symbolic* sense.[55]

---

54. The use of the word "market" in this sentence is used to consolidate all the various actors within such a space: citizens, consumers, corporations, etc.
55. The use of the word "becomes" is used out of simplicity and convenience; it is necessary to question whether money was ever more then an illusion of value. In this way money has not become an illusion. Instead, money is, and has always been, an illusion - a mirror - to an otherwise opaque force.

Item 3: Fable Uncovered

I

With one complete circle traced, this discussion now finds itself at its starting point - examining the connection between money and value once more. For clarity, the circumference examined should be recapitulated: the fundamental purpose of a monetary economy is to create objects that are valuable and, because objects are produced and do not fall out of the sky, human input (labor) is intrinsically necessary to create a valuable object. This is a Marxist claim that is not political but structural; a commodity's origin is its laborer and, as was raised at the outset of this work, the goats that *you* shepherded are valuable because *you* (as a goat herder) put in months of time tending to them.[1]

There is no getting around this. Labor is a location of value.[2] And this common denominator of labor, that all objects share, allows them to be comparable to each other. Once more we return to the goats. When *you* traded one of your goats for 5 sheets of wood (and did not use the device of money as an intermediary in the exchange) the third commodity of labor was able to translate the worth of both these items into the language of value; you have claimed that the labor-value of one goat is equal to the labor-value of 5 sheets of wood. The introduction of money changes nothing other than easing the object-to-value translation; money makes physical the element of labor that is already concealed at the time of trade.[3]

---

1. The political claim is that because laborers are the engine of capitalism - because they are the force that allows for the production of value - they must be provided with honorable salaries that are directly linked with the sale price of an item. Further, the political argument asserts that the price of a commodity (or its exchange value) should be a display of the commodity's cost of production with a minimal amount of deviation. While this political stance is enticing, this paper is not political and it is for this reason that such claims will not be engaged and critiqued. However, it is difficult to refute the structural claim that labor is a vital input in the creation of a commodity - that without labor a commodity could not be brought to market for sale. [Refer to Item I, part II for this original example.]
2. "a" and not "the" is used here for a reason that will quickly become evident.
3. One could argue that modern forms of money (like credit cards, bank accounts that only exist on computer screens and stock markets to name a few) are not physical. While modern money forms are no doubt digital, they are still objects that can be seen, visualized, and owned.

Such a structuralist[4] claim incorrectly interprets the contemporary economy, or stated with more empathy for Marx, the systematic claims made around value being the sole product of labor do not appropriately define the functions of value or money.[5] The monetary price at which an item is sold has never been in direct correlation with its labor cost. Instead, additional elements beyond labor govern the value of an object; among other forces, the perceived use, the socially produced desire and the demand for an object can alter the monetary value associated with a commodity. There is no getting around this either; value is a labyrinth - an intricate and opaque combination of elements that are in flux and

---

4. At this point the words "structural" and "structuralist" have been used. They should simplify this discussion, and not make it more complex. The invocation of such a root term should not be linked to the structuralist movement - or to its recognizable thinkers: Claude Lévi-Strauss, Louis Althusser and Jacques Lacan. Simply stated for clarity: the claim that Marx mobilizes is that commodities are the product of labor, that the genealogy of every object starts with production - in either a physical or mental form, and that because of this every object can only be worth the cost of production. The claim need not be attached to an ideology - that structures are the *real things* that lie beneath the surface or the appearance of meaning. When this word is invoked at other points in this work, it should be interpreted with such a limited purpose.

5. It is also important to understand the conclusions that a strict Marxist reading would bring; if labor were solely producing the implied (or recognized) value of an object, then all objects would have to be diametrically reevaluated to be monetarily worth the cost of production. (The Marxist definition of "cost-of-production" does take into account more than the cost of labor. It also accounts for the cost of the factory, tools, and any other element that was physically involved in the production process of a commodity.)

un-calculable, not a list of locatable elements such as labor.[6] It is at this point that an irreconcilable contradiction emerges. Value is a complex and unique force inside of an object; the symbol of money that has come to define it is the inverse. Money is simple and seemingly transparent; money candidly proclaims an object's value with the universally recognized language of quantities and units.[7]

Because money presents itself as gifted at deciphering the illusive quality of value,[8] it is able to make a claim to be a finality. Objects with an exchange-value[9] are a finished project for an economy - they have a value (in the monetary sense) and they can be exchanged with one another based on a singular framework. Nothing in this schema is in question. In fact money works as a *universal signifier* - an arbitrary yet historically significant and pervasive symbol that is able to represent, and signify, all else around it.[10] Friedrich Engels terms money *the commodity of commodities,* an object that can "...hold all other commodities

---

6. To give Marx his credit he did develop a category for these non-labor forces that produce value - this is the category of surplus value. Surplus value is the profit a capitalist enjoys after paying out for the cost of production; it is equal to the net sum of retained earnings that are not payed out to laborers meaning that surplus value is, in a Marxist sense, the product of worker exploitation. Further, this excess value that is infused into a commodity is the result of capitalists allowing (or forcing) their products to be sold above the cost of production; consumers will buy items at these inflated prices because, again, as a Marxist would state, a market can valorize or fetishize products. Beyond the political thrust of such an argument (that quickly becomes engaged with labor rights and not economic anthropology), Marx still has value operating as a calculation - Marx would not say that the value of any objects is a mystery, unfindable, or in debate, just that the market has exploited labor to produce an altered exchange value for a commodity.

7. To expand on this distinction, it is crucial to appreciate that money is not value, but a device that consolidates the complexities and uniqueness of an object's value into a singular statement and, in doing so, becomes the means of evaluation. Value is not inside of these "things" - these social tools like fiat paper, bank notes, minted coins, and markings on a personal dwelling; money is of a different quality.

8. Illusive to everyone but Marx.

9. The socially accepted price point at which an item can be bought or sold; a monetary nomenclature that is, in theory, derived from an object's use value.

10. Jean-Joseph Goux, a thinker whose ideas will be put to immense use in this section, uses the term "general equivalent" to identify this same notion.

hidden [inside of] itself."[11] Jacques Derrida[12] will soon be invoked below and insists upon a similar notion: that Marx's economy, made up of an 'immense accumulation of commodities', is in fact only a vast space of signs all reliant on a singular symbol - money - for meaning and recognizable worth. The hierarchical chart that Derrida builds plainly describes the relationship between money, an object, and value. At its base is the device of money that has been granted social prowess to flatten the labyrinth of value into a singular statement. Built on such a base is the sum of an economy's commodities that are evaluated by the signifier of money, resulting in a network of objects all labeled and defined solely though this numerical device. Unitizing money, or any singular device to describe value, is problematic on these very grounds because the use of such an instrument consolidates the complex force of value around a singular notion and, in the process, leaves elements out.[13]

This reading of the marketplace presents a scenario where all commodities are networked to each other though their relationship with money. It also means that money does not produce an ending point of value but only a verification or a sonar signal for the value inside of an object.[14] Its seems, then, that money is operating in a linguistic fashion in the sense that money

---

11. Friedrich Engels was a 19th century social and political theorist who was a close friend of Marx. Together they produced The Communist Manifesto in 1848. Engels also edited the second and third volumes of Das Kapital after Marx's death. [Engels, 1972, *Origin* (p.225).]
12. Jacques Derrida was a French philosopher who lived from 1930 to 2004. His work has profoundly impacted philosophical thought; he is known as the founder of deconstructionism. The invocation of Derrida's name, to a segment of readers, conjures a mountain of thought and for this reason the goal will be to speak about him with clarity.
13. Any device or signifier (including labor) cannot adequately define, explain, or consolidate the forces of value accurately.
14. Sonar is a deep sea device used by vessels that need to calculate the position and distances of surrounding objects by bouncing a sound wave off the object in question and then solving for distances based on the time it took for the sound wave to return to the vessel multiplied by the speed of sound. Money and commodities are in a similar tussle; money, in a sense, checks for value like a doctor checks for the pulse of his patient.

describes an object, but solely through the use of numerical units. Moreover, money as a linguistic device inhabits the space of the "third" commodity - that Marx insisted was labor - in an accomplished act of placing objects in relation to each other with these same numerical units. Accompanying this with a concrete example will be helpful: When a bank defends the value of its reserves, when a government claims its currency is sound and stable, when a company markets its new fangled product as more valuable than other comparable items, or when a friend says their house is worth a certain amount, the words of money, not other objects of value, sustain their arguments. This is because the *value* of an object is always concealed, hidden, and only representable by a device that can bridge such a gap.

In sum, the instrument of money is the crucial element of a capitalist economy; it is simply that money is laying claim to a force - value - that has been historically anchored to an object but, in truth, categorically unrelated to it. In doing so money is coding objects with a *fiction of value* - a fiction that an object's value can be, has, and continues to be, successfully defined with the aid of a universal signifier.

II.

Now the usefulness of money is becoming clear; money is the acclaimed device that links commodities together, translates value into a universal language of numbers, and excavates the value of any object for the economy to see, hold, and trade. But while money is the annunciator of value, its proclamations are translations of dynamic objects whose values change.[15] A Marxist would claim that the true value[16] of a commodity can only be altered if the raw costs of production change, but the perceived value - and therefor the object-to-money translation - is governed by more than these principles. And while there are numerous exemplars of this point, the financial industry has been a consistent refrain in this work, so a return to it once more is justified. Let's pick February 4, 2010, a day when the Dow Jones Industrial Average dropped a massive 268 points (a more then 3% move) and Steve Grasso, a sales trader for Stuart Frankel, which places orders for large pension funds, mutual funds and hedge funds on the floor of the New York Stock Exchange, was interviewed on cable television:

"There was a lot of fear on the floor today; people did not know what to do; everyone was so confused; Guys did not know what they wanted to do. I look at it like this: the amount of IM's I got on the floor, or the amounts of hits I get, with people saying 'what is going on, what are you seeing'; I had by 9:35[am] 150 IM's hitting me, flooding me, 'what's it you're seeing, what's gong on', and it only cascaded higher, not lower, as the day

---

15. An office building is a prime example. The cost to build an office building does not reflect the social or marketplace value of that proprety; a plethora of other factors do. The properties adjacent to it, the area of the city, the tenants that occupy it and how well the property has been maintained are just some of these factors. But the best proof that the value of an object is dynamic is that people fight over an object's value in an effort to translate value into the language of money. This is why a bidding war could break out for a property or why a seller will insist upon a higher sale price - because each actor interprets (or translates) value differently. The value of an object is not clear cut, it is fluctuating and elusive.

16. The Marxist term is actually "use value". The market value (or the monetary value) of an object is considered its "exchange value".

progressed. Guys were hitting me more and more and more."[17]

Mr. Grasso is proclaiming a change in value that has nothing to do with fundamental-based data or the costs of production. Instead, he locates emotion as the cause for the negative revaluation of the broad market. In turn, the quality of value is not only in excess of labor but in excess of a singular quality or heuristic - it is malleable, unstable, dynamic and unique to each item. The claim is not that Mr. Grasso has located the true governor of value, only that he has noticed a shift in value; he has found an additional source of value (emotion) and countless more can be found.

In so much as money is the language deployed to speak of value, its readings are a vast oversimplification of such a complex element. In turn, the term *value*, as a capitalist economy wishes to contextualize it, is a fiction; value is always misspoken of in terms of a *standardized tool* - always thought of as only a matter of units or monetary symbols.[18] Further, a claim of an object's value, while structured as an absolute, is in fact only a claim[19] to an amount of money an object can be traded for, which is always in flux. If this proclamation comes as an erratic claim, it is for the reason that Mark Twain identified in 1898 when he proclaimed that "[t]ruth is stranger than fiction... because fiction is obliged to stick to possibilities, truth isn't."[20]

Mark Twain defined a fiction as a story that must be coherent, and it is this very rule that the fiction of value abides by -

17. This is a direct, non abbreviated transcription. [Word on the Street (CNBC news channel), 2010, *Steven Grasso*.]
18. Value, within the factious network of capitalism, is a repetition of the same ideal across all objects as opposed to a singular device that is presentable. Such a distinction, between a singularity and a standard, is important to this work; to say that value singular is to claim that value is a unique, non-duplicative, device - it is the opposite. Value is pervasive - it can be conceptualized as a pattern that is copied onto objects with relentless ease.
19. This could also be understood as a fictional reference.
20. Twain, 1898, *Following* (p.156).

he rule that money is the sole tool for value translation.[21] This rule s a code - an intricate list of formulas that generates monetary symbols for each of the world's commodities.[22] This code forms an endless network of objects that are all connected to money because they all operate within its structure; simultaneously, this network is self validating - collectively breathing meaning and exchangeable value into all objects. Finally, this network takes the form of a globalized map - a territorialized environment of objects that have been pre-interpreted with the signifier of money.[23] When this[24] environment is proclaimed as fictitious both its effectiveness and its power are fully accounted for. For a fiction is simultaneously powerful; a fiction constructs a world that makes sense, that is self validating, that operates with minimal disruption and evades questioning. And in this way monetary value is purposefully producing a structured world around a factious concept.

III.

It would be easy to claim that money is a fiction because it is just a piece of paper. This is evident, so this is not the claim. Instead this work's interests lie in the *simulacrum* that money

---

21. At some level this should be clear; monetary economies are a fiction. They operate because they can claim they have found unquestionable truths - this simply cannot be.
22. Jean Baudrillard terms this system the "structural law of value". [Baudrillard, 1993, *Symbolic.*]
23. The notion of a map is fundamental to both this inquiry and to numerous thinkers. Maps are the product of civilization - they are vast tomes of knowledge. Maps are a cartography - a network of signifiers that give an account of the world.
24. The words, "our", "American", "a monetary economy", "a capitalist" and a host of many more are easily interchangeable with this word.

produces.[25] For what money[26] truly does is materialize the absences, the non-translatability, of value. To produce this simulacrum, the tale that value can be reincarnated into a monetary device must be historically anchored; everything discussed in the first two sections concerned this same fiction.[27] Most important to this narrative was the backstop that gold - the patriarchal universal signifier - provided to the process of exchange.

The dominant account holds that gold, unlike every other commodity, is somehow an objective or raw asset of value, external to the monetary systems of society and forever protected from degradation. But ask yourself, "how real is that value of gold? Is it not simply a yellowish metal?"[28] The version of history that has been propagated for gold is neither accurate nor philosophically supported and, as Karl Marx writes:

> *"[N]ature no more produces [gold] than it does bankers or discount rates. But since the capitalist system of production requires the crystallization of wealth as a fetish in the form of a single article, gold and silver appear as its appropriate incarnation. [...] But the capacity of a particular*

---

25. This work, however, is not interested in decoding the endless list of elements that make up an object's value. The goal of the work is simply to map and explain how a monetary economy is sustained solely on the premise of a universal signifier creating a simulacrum of knowledge. The term "simulacrum" is from the writings of Plato and means "a likeness, image or representation." The definition incorporates an inherent sense of the unreality or of the vagueness of the representation. [Plato, 2007, *Republic*.]
26. It should be clear at this point that the term money is a global term for all monetary signifiers. Money is equivalent to gold, fiat paper and the multitude of other random objects that monetary systems use for their universal signifier of value.
27. After reading this final chapter return to the beginning again; the detailed explanations on the inner workings of the economy were descriptions of the fiction of value.
28. Critchley, 2009, *Coins* (New York Times opinion section).

commodity to serve as a universal equivalent...
[is] a social result of the process of exchange. "[29]

Marx was well aware that money could never be anything other then a signifier and translator of value. In doing so, Marx aligns himself with an entire host of thinkers who conceptualize money as merely a device that all objects use for evaluation.[30] For much of gold's history, before it was quietly decoupled from American fiat in 1971 by the Nixon administration, its valuable status was unquestioned, not because its value was identifiable, but because a fascinating mythology was built around it - that its presence and ownership was valuable in and of itself.

Such folklore is of the utmost importance to civilizations that use a universal signifier as the mechanism of evaluation, because it is the historicity and longevity of the universal signifier of value that also sustains this signifier's power. Looking back to the invention of the American dollar, which is just the latest incarnation of a universal signifier, this proves true; invented in 1775, it took the American people and the nation's banks over 150 years to establish trust and faith in the monetary device of the American dollar.[31] It was only after dollars could be socially trusted to correctly translate value that this currency took hold. To reiterate, monetary economies develop and expand because of

29. Marx, 1859, *Contributions* (p.48).
30. The claim is also that the device of money can be anything. It does not have to be yellow rocks; it could be green paper, white shells, or black crosses. In addition, for clarity, the entire host of thinkers Marx aligns himself with are, conveniently, the thinkers this work itself favors.
31. For more history refer to Item 1, part II.

these devices, and not the inverse; these master signifiers are constructed out of necessity and not in error.[32]

With the historical location of money in place it is now evident that, despite an economy's consistent effort to argue otherwise, "money is a symbol of value" because money has always been a tool that testifies for value. But this means that money is not the site of value, but, using a term borrowed from Jacques Derrida, *the trace of value*; money operates like value's derivative - a copy that does not retain the essence of its parent and is in this way hollow.[33] "[T]he trace is not a presence but the simulacrum of a presence that dislocates itself, displaces itself, refers [to] itself...[;]its property has no site...[.]"[34] This truth is not lofty but practical - what is gold, dollars, credit cards, a bank account on a computer screen, or the unrealized gains from stock trading activities displayed on a financial statement if not the trace of value, the outline of it, the testament to value that cannot otherwise be spoken of with such universality?

Those who claim to be wealthy because they have accumulated large amounts of dollars affirm that society is unaware what value truly is. But this is the power of the universal signifier at work - American dollars need not display the multitude of factors that were used to translate value into the language of money, only that such a task was completed with great care for the benefit of universal exchange with other objects. The dilemma is one of unauthorized links between the value moving inside of an object (which is unique) and money (a standardized tool). When

---

32. John Smith speaks to a similar notion. He writes: "... the textbook story about money emerging spontaneously from some pre-existing natural economy based on barter is rejected as being both historically and logically inaccurate. Rather than money emerging from the market, the suggestion is that if anything the converse is true." The claim is that money allows objects be be placed in relation to each other and that such relationships are necessary to sustain a scalable social environment. [Smith, 2000, *What* (p.4).]
33. The contextualization of the term "derivative" is derived, in part, from the work of Edward LiPuma. [LiPuma, 2004, *Financial.*]
34. Derrida, 1985, *Margins* (p.24).

money lays claim to bridging this gap, it does so through *misdirection*. Again, Derrida speaks to such a concept:

> *"[W]hen we cannot grasp or show the thing [value], state the present, [or] the being-present, when the present cannot be presented, we signify, we go through the detour of the sign. We take or give signs, we signal. The sign, in this sense, is deferred presence."*[35]

For Derrida the circulation of money proclaims a deferral - a workaround - in the evaluation of an object's value; because when money translates value it also acts as though it has done so with precision which is not the case. Instead, money is a detour to the understanding of value - always one step away from it - a space that, in truth, cannot be located with money.

A clear structure is being built that must be elucidated in order to move forward. The device of money, gold or otherwise, is not value but the translator of value which has been authorized to decipher value because of a historicity and mythology built into it. Giving an object a monetary value provides an object with universally recognized social meaning; because value is illusive and unique to every commodity it is seemingly made transparent, and transposed into a standardized form, with the device of money; finally, money is not value but a detour or misdirection of value.[36]

---

35. Derrida, 1985, Margins (p.9).
36. A small digression can be made with this point; what is fascinating about this standardized form of value is that it is allowed, within the network of capitalism, to produce (to accumulate) more value (more of itself) through such a misdirection. As monetary value cycles through this detour - in the hunt for the unique makeup of an object - it builds on itself. In this way the more difficult it is to find an object's uniqueness, the more valuable this vary object is perceived to be. Take the lofty notion of a financial derivative - its value is so illusive, so hidden within a complex network of financial actors, that it attracts the wildest, and highest, predictions of its monetary value. But, conversely, an apple has the perception of simplicity (that is historically produced) that produces a lesser socially recognized accumulation of value.

IV.

The world's commodities are collapsing onto each other; the differences between commodities are becoming trivial because all commodities are evaluated by the same signifier. Fiat money, the universal signifier of value, is becoming the "...metaphor for the transcendental guarantee of meaning."[37] What fascinates Jean-Joseph Goux, when he makes such a claim, is the ability for a single word - value - to breath meaning into every other item.[38] And to be clear, a specific type of value: value as defined by money. Such an assertion rivals the de-facto premise of a monetary economy. The assertion is that while every item is presented and perceived as unique they are in fact not; that a monetary economy is the upkeep of only a singular symbol - money - that is universal in its function and the sole sustenance of every object.[39] And this "...symbol is a visible substitute that replaces something hidden [value], something that is not presentable."[40] This is the truth, but the *fiction of value* must posit the inverse. Our economic environment, that runs on a fiction of value, must vehemently assert that while all objects are monetarily defined they can still be classified as unique.[41]

---

37. Goux, 1990, *Symbolic* (p.103).
38. Goux, in the same vein of this work, uses the term value in the monetary sense.
39. This principle should be further outlined but has been footnoted for reasons of simplicity. When Goux posits that the economy is only the upkeep of the singular symbol of money he is speaking to the fact that all objects have become only their numerical counterparts. A $20 TV and a $50 shirt are just physical states of the same device - money: first as $20 and then as $50. In making such a claim all objects become abstractions of their physicality. This argument is compelling because the individual who has $70 may obtain both these items listed above with ease; he just uses $70 to acquire $20 and $50. The claim is that an economy is just, in the end, these monetary symbols. And this is why the fiction of value must posit the inverse - this fiction must claim that every object remains distinct and unique while being monetarily valuable.
40. Goux, 1990, Symbolic (p.124).
41. It should be becoming clear that this is impossible; if a group of objects are defined by a standardized hubristic they have then become the opposite of unique - objects are then mundane, duplicative and repetitive.

This is precisely what Milton Friedman seeks to accomplish when he claims that a monetary economy is made up of numerous components and not a singular symbol displaying itself in different states or quantities. Friedman's most acclaimed notion is that a capitalist economy is an engine powering the world; that such an engine cannot be photographed, understood or spoken of in one breath; that neither value nor money are consolidations of other complex components.[42] Capitalism is *an engine not a camera* - a Friedman follower would say.[43] In such a reading money is not conducting a translation of value but merely placing value, in an unaltered state, on display. For those who follow Friedman - for a *monetareolist*[44] - the ideology in this credo is clear: value is a calculation and not a substance made up of human emotions, neurologically produced instruments or other non-calculable elements. Instead, the free market is a space of countless items which can be accurately measured with mathematical equations; in turn these equations are able to precisely value the net sum of the world's commodities. To acquiesce to a monetareolist's alluring fable is to accept that an economy is only understandable through the gaze of data, and that data can tabulate value.

This glorified proclamation is also the proof of the fiction of value. To debunk Friedman with the use of his own terminology, how can the value of the market be tabulated, calculated and traded without forcing everything to be evaluated by a singular signifier - such as money? If Friedman's credo is one of complexity - that the free market is beyond a photographic deduction of knowledge - then the ability for data to precisely value, and express, the net sum

---

42. This work will land on the other side of this argument; capitalism - monetary economies - are sustained only by a *fiction of value*.

43. This claim is laid out with clarity in Friedman's theory of "positive economics" [Friedman, 1966, *Positive*]

44. A "monetareolist" is a generally accepted term in the economic community for a person who aligns him/her self with the work of Milton Friedman. Monetarism is the view that variation in the money supply within an economy will significantly influence the value of the economy as a whole - in short that money matters, is real, is a calculation of value, and is a truly valuable object.

of the world's commodities is discontinuous with such a self imposed philosophy. And if the universal signifier of money is the weapon of choice to tabulate the value of the market, then it does hold that a monetary economy is *a camera, not an engine*. A camera in the sense that the use of money to tabulate value produces an ultimate or photographic gaze - a number that can make a singular declarative statement for the worth of an entire economy or an individual object.[45] The use of this gaze is one of simplicity and singularity, as Jean-Joseph Goux raised above; in a singular breath: all items are being tagged with monetary nomenclatures and then valued.

The truth is that this evaluation is incomplete or incorrect; or as Donald MacKenzie argues: to claim that such an apparatus like capitalism is measuring to perfection *the market* "...is clearly as much an impossibility as a map that reproduces exactly every aspect and feature of terrain and landscape."[46] The undeniable truth is that this capitalistic gaze is fictitious, not because such an apparatus is incapable of tabulating value, but because such a system claims that money and data can do so without error - without leaving elements out. To assert this masterful victory, such a gaze must label every object with money, meaning that every commodity must be consolidated, in the world of monetareolist data, as an idealized and symbolic object. This is what Jean-Joseph Goux is asserting a monetary economy has always been; when the urge is to acknowledge all objects in terms of their monetary value, then they only exist in an abstract fashion. In such a space only a *symbolic economy* is present and not the fictional machine Friedman triumphed; in such a space the real has been replaced by the symbolic.

---

45. The use of the concept "ultimate gaze" is directly taken from Michel Foucault's 1963 book "The Birth of the Clinic" where Foucault first lays out the framework for the systematic way in which systems (such as a clinic or the medical community) produce irrefutable knowledge, or an ultimate gaze. These claims are later reframed in his subsequent work, "The Order Of Things".
46. MacKenzie, 2008, *Engine* (p.11).

To be clear, when a *gaze* is employed in the tabulation of value it is the universal signifier of money that authorizes such a calculation. For Goux the goal, in a relationship between money (the signifier) and value (the calculation), is to focus "... exclusively on the results and not the process, which includes tensions, imbalances, discrepancies, and an internal creative tendency toward an equilibrium that is never achieved."[47] Goux views a monetary economy as one that yearns to produce an ultimate answer, wishes to speak from within a singular statement, and is always building a simulacrum of meaning from a lonely notion. To further this realization an additional statement must be added: the maintenance of a space made only of variations of the same idea - to retain a social environment made up of only monetarily valuable objects - prohibits a space from engaging in anything other than calculations.

V.

All that remains is a notion of value; such a notion is inescapable. But one must be careful when using this term because *value* is split into two forms. The first is the calculable, fictitious from of value - a monetary value, a universally recognizable value. The second is *valeur*[48] - a substance that is made of an immense number of components. And while this substance cannot guard against the forces of money, it remains beyond calculation. Such a distinction is made in a final effort to separate fact from fiction. For while Friedman, neoclassical economists, and the monetary economy itself argue that these two forms of value are one and the same, or that only the former exists, in truth they are radically

47. Goux, 1990, *Symbolic* (p.128).
48. Valeur is best defined as an excess - the category of the singularity that is always multiplicative because its form is always unique to each item, beyond an anchored definition and uncapturable by a universal signifier.

different. Value is a fictitious calculation, while *valeur* is in excess of such a principle.

The truth is that value, to conduct evaluation, to be evaluated, to use value to determine the meaning or worth of an object, is not only the sole process of a monetary economy, it is also the production of a fiction because it claims to define a force - valeur - that it categorically cannot define. Further, this task - to excavate the value of an item - is the sole mission of monetarily bound citizens. And with necessity, for it is when an object has value that it can also have universal meaning. With this very acknowledgment - that the notion of value can subsequently code an object - one finds the hoax of value. While value is irrefutably singular it is categorized as multiplicative. The notion of value is able to fabricate objects that claim to have distinct properties, identities and qualities. This statement is the annunciation of a fiction; the truth is that all commodities are not unique but standardized elements, meaning that every object of value is nothing more than *an object of value* with no further distinction available to it. To defend such an assertion, however, supporting arguments should be laid out.

Our world has been constructed out of a singular symbol - the universal symbol of money - that every object has succumbed to. This is more than problematic, it is the discovery of a rigged, confining, simplistic, predetermined space; an environment of forces that neatly falls into place because they all have been deduced to a singular quality. The system can be synthesized as follows: all commodities of a monetary economy are labeled with value, acclaimed through a relationship with money, and differentiated by a catalogue of verbalizable differences.

It is this last step - the verbalization of countless differences that allows value's fiction to flourish; such proclamations[49] of an item's uniqueness fabricates objects that can simultaneously be monetarily valuable while ostensibly distinct. In truth, the variations between commodities concerns only their implied value.[50] If differences between objects remain noticeable[51] the source of such distinctions is the *différance* that persists.[52] When Derrida states that "'[d]ifférance' is the non-full, non-simple, structured and differentiating origin of differences[,]"[53] he is consolidating an entire discourse into a singular factual statement.[54]

---

49. One could name the differences between two objects for quite some time: the differences in color, size, weight, material, construction, vintage, design; the list is endless. In the end, all these possible variations arrive at a singular statement: an object's monetary value.

50. Such a statement could be perceived incorrectly. For example, that all works of art are the same work but with different numerical values attached. To be sure, works of art have substantial variance (their color pallette, composition, provocativeness, maker, to name just a few). But all art (and all commodities) cannot escape the process of evaluation. This means that all works of art areunder the gaze of a monetary economy, the same object - the same object at different price points.

51. If you still think that your goats are a distinctly different object than the wood that can be traded for it.

52. Meaning that a singular notion creates the "countless variances" displayed in commodities.

53. Derrida, 1985, *Margins* (*p.*16).

54. The introduction of the term différance could be interpreted as an aside to the main conversation. This work is, in part, re-appropriating the term "différance" because it was originally employed around discourses involving language; it is a a combination of the word differ and defer. Take "able" and "table" where the only difference is the symbol "t". But this small difference generates an entirely new meaning for the word presented. In light of this, it seems that the 26 symbols of the English alphabet can form an inordinate number of words and meanings - especially when full words are placed next to each other. The claim, for this work, is that money acts in this same linguistic fashion as the alphabet but with only 10 symbols (0,1,2,3,4,5,6,7,8,9). But from these symbols large differences are formed; because a string like $384.77 invokes a vastly different connotation than the string of $901,842,161.75. This is différance - the differences that are formed from a base set of possible permutations; that when these symbols are placed together they form seemingly distinct objects that differ one from the other but still refer to the base symbols for their meaning. Reading this section again, after this knowledge, will be helpful.

An explanation of such a point remains necessary; the catalogue of verbalizable differences available between objects is always employed to find and settle on a monetary price and so the work of differentiating between objects is more accurately the work of linking them together - allowing every object to be described solely through the use of money. To be clear, the only difference between objects is the monetary *différance* between them. Said yet another way: when one claims that a goat is white with four legs and that a sheet of wood is dark brown and thin, these differences form connotations of value where each difference is worth a designated numerical unit. In turn, the origin of an object's perceived uniqueness is its value - its physical qualities merely aid in finding such a calculation.

An endless loop has been formed - money defines a commodity and a commodity is defined by money. Both use the other as a reference to their definition or their most elementary form.[55] These connections quickly become confusing and for Jean Baudrillard, this is precisely the point. For him, value operates as a mirror of itself, with no original form or location. "The modern sign dreams of its predecessor, and would dearly love to rediscover an obligation in its reference to the real [to *valeur*]. It finds only a reason, a referential reason, a 'real' and a 'natural' on which it will feed."[56] A return to our humble goats plainly elucidates this point. When a goat is valued at $5 it has acquiesced to a price point, making it no different from any other object of value, but more importantly its price is a mirror of all the goats before it - the $5 sign of value is referring to an endless historical line of identical

---

55. This point is best grounded with a practical circumstance. Take the purchase of a house. One could say "this house is worth $500,000" or "$500,000 will grant you ownership to this property". In the former statement the house is the reference point to the $500,000; in the latter the $500,000 is the reference point to the house.
56. Baudrillard, 1993, *Symbolic* (p.51).

objects that also were successfully labeled with value.[57] Here, in such an economy, the justification for value's presence is the historical line of objects that were successfully valued. In doing so, an object's value is merely a counterfeit of its predecessors with an inability to locate the original - or *real* - object of *valeur*.

Now the presumption that value is even real is being questioned. What remains defendable is that an object's historicity as a commodity of value is the source of the contemporary claims of worth attached to it. But when Baudrillard states that "value rules according to an ungraspable order"[58] he is consolidating such a history of valuable objects and noticing that no foundation - or start point - emerges.[59] Instead, this endless network of valuable objects exists ungrounded in an economy, strung together with money. The proper visual representation is one of a circle where all objects lay side by side, glued together only with the quality of monetary value. Such a heuristic generates an *ungraspable order* because the linguistic work of money, which has a *"monopoly on signification"*,[60] does not display the process of evaluation - only the completion of such a task. It is around this structural device of money that Baudrillard and Goux dance. Baudrillard's work finds that "...the common denominator of the real world... is the signifier [and not a more foundational element]... that refers to a disenchanted universe of the signified."[61] Goux's work caries this argument to its next logical point, that this universe of signified objects is strung together with the glue of money that "...makes

57. This is a simplification. The price point of any object, in this case goats, does fluctuate, and most likely increases, over time. However, the accusation that the accepted worth of these goats is based on a history of valuable goats that have no identifiable start (or commencement point) remains. When an item is valued its value is a product of history.
58. Baudrillard, 1993, *Symbolic* (p.3).
59. Why, at its most fundamental level, is a goat worth $5? Think about it: is it not because the goats raised last year were labeled (and successfully sold) at virtually the identical price? The answer is unequivocally yes.
60. Goux, 1990, *Symbolic* (p.170).
61. Baudrillard, 1993, *Symbolic* (p.50).

viable a purely symbolic order, in that it appears to be founded solely on complex linkage[s] and diacritical determination."[62]

Such an argument finds a static universal signifier which supports a network of commodities all wishing to levy the same singular, claim - the claim that they are in fact valuable. Such a fiction of value provides objects with the mechanism to proclaim a value and remain visually distinct.

VI.

To continue further, at such a stage in this discourse, would not yield further revelations - only more explanations for the same set of proclamations; what has been boldly elucidated is the fiction of value that supports all monetary societies. It is a fiction that allows all objects to be defined by a singular universal signifier while allowing each to remain distinguishable; it is a fiction that idealizes the notion of value and, by doing so, provides the capabilities to speculate, and profit, on future forms of value; it is a fiction that is founded on a history of valuable objects that have been successfully traded because of their standard, and universally recognizable characteristics.

From the start,[63] we have lived in an idealized system of value where, in so much as objects exist, they present themselves as unified, organized and congruent. Karl Marx was insistent that the base of such a stunning system was labor. While he is correct - objects cannot be brought to market without labor, the functionality of such a system relies on all objects being deducible to a different denominator[64] - the symbols of money and the proclamation of universal value. Any economy and social environment - the fictitious city of Capitalville noted at the beginning of this work or otherwise - was never about building an apparatus that produced

---

62. Goux, 1990, *Symbolic* (p.49).
63. From the birth of the first universal signifier.
64. The truth is that laborers make commodities, they don't make valeur.

ruths, but one that could operate efficiently by commanding a *listinctive gaze*. When banks, governments, capitalists and consumers live in a world were monetary value serves as route of ill things, each operates within a fiction of value. The truth of these systems, as Derrida writes, is something else entirely. "What is liscovered... is that there is no nucleus of meaning, no conceptual itom, but that the concept is produced within the tissue of lifferences."[65]   Found in Jacques Derrida's writings is the realization that there is, in fact, no faithful master signifier but only lifferences between objects that have been created by such a levice.

If one is to critique the premise of universally recognized monetary value, it is through this avenue: the ultimate purpose of a capitalist society is to define everything and anything with a price point in an effort to trade and understand that object only through the meaning its price point produces. In turn, the fiction of value is the production of perfection; it is a claim that an object is completely - without mistake - definable, understandable and calculable. In such an ultimate claim money is the agent of perfection. It is the device that has made all objects the same. One must realize that the goal of society is the production of pre-packaged meaning - a category that a fiction can find and that a truth can not.[66]

---

65. Derrida, 1980, *Writing* (p.276).
66. This is the beginning of a much larger project. In an important, yet repetitive, exercise a laundry list of empirical sites and historical events could now be invoked to display the fiction of value. In fact, the historical sites that would be brought to the forefront of this discussion (the list of topics could be: stock market crashes, corporate bankruptcies, world trading networks, and the exchange rates of sovereign currencies) would display an inconsistency in the perceived perfect apparatus this fiction of value has built. But such a conversation is not directly linked to this work, so this paper will end here, to allow a new project to begin. Using what has been discussed in this work as a foundation, there is an opportunity to provide commentary (what can also be termed "thick description") on events within the emblem of an economy. It is for this exact reason that this work will end; it will be allowed to breathe on its own terms.

VII. Additions

Nothing is left to speak too and yet an additional - a supplemental - peace of writing is being added.[67]

To speak of a universal signifier, and the fiction of value that authorizes its use, is not theoretical - these elucidated forms are pervasive. One such ethnographic site is the 2007 financial crisis and the failure of Lehman Brothers, a global financial services company that boasted the year before of its $503.5 billion in net assets and $4 billion of profits in its annual report.[68] The question becomes one of simplicity: how could over $500 billion of money disappear in as little as a few months; what actions would allow such a quantity of universally recognized symbols of value to be lost or misplaced; how was this firm left with no choice but to declare bankruptcy? Financial analysts have framed this bank failure as one of poor oversight, the result of excessive risk taking, and an inability to properly hedge against the financial investments being made. This work posits that what was behind this failure is something far more primal.

Lehman Brothers failed because it was unable to sustain the perception of its own value - it could not continue to produce a fiction of value. And in tenuous moments during a congressional hearing two years later in 2010, Richard Fuld, the Chief Executive Officer at Lehman Brothers during the collapse, aligns himself with this exact stance. "We had collateral, we had capital, but... the world believed that there was a capital hole [at our firm]. So for those that thought that it was [*that we were*] thirty [billion dollars in debt] it was [*we were*] [...]"[69] The comments by Mr. Fuld affirm

---

67. In the previous footnote it was suggested that such a continuance would not take place. This "additions section" should not be considered part of the main work. It is an ad-on; a proof of concept that thick description can be conducted on an ethnographic event.

68. Fuld, *Lehman 2007 Annual Report* (p.4).

69. House Financial Services Committee. Hearing on Lehman Bros Report, 111th Congress Cong.

hat, above all else, the financial collapse was the failure of a belief system - an inability to successfully defend the value of his assets under management. A dialogue with Joe Donnelley, a Republican congressman representing the 2nd District of Indiana, drives at this same point:

> Donnelley: "You have said that it was not a capital hole, that the capital was there. That you had the 26 [billion dollars in liquidity]. What was it then [that made Lehman fail]. Was it a loss of confidence? Why did we wake up and see Lehman gone?"
> Fuld: "I think it was a loss of confidence. [...] I think that we could not convince the world that, about, the condition we were in; that we had collateral, that we had capital, we had a solid plan. [Mr. Fuld stops and then starts a new sentence] We could not convince the world of our solvency."

The ideology that is the fiction of value, which allows all objects, and in this case financial assets, to be valued with the universal signifier of money, is only as useful as a belief in the capabilities for such a credo. In this way the financial crisis is just that - a crisis in the faith the market has constructed for the value of objects. Mr. Fuld is saying nothing more than the observation that the market had lost faith in Lehman's value; he is realizing that the fiction his firm had meticulously constructed over the last 150 years [70] - that Lehman was equipped to value exotic assets with a universal signifier and make profits off their trade - had collapsed.

A financial crisis, then, is an impasse in our markets' fiction of value. It is a short lived episode - a hiccup - in the ability for money to defend the value and meaning of our society's objects. It is a crisis in the senses that these moments make transparent the

---

70. Fuld, *Lehman 2007 Annual Report* (p.3)

financial system to display that value is derived from a confidence - from a form of blind faith - in money's capabilities. Jacques-Alair Miller, a Lacanian scholar, concurs with such a reading:

"In short, there is crisis in the psychoanalytical sense, when speech, discourse, the words, the figures, the rites, the routine, all the symbolic apparatus, prove suddenly impotent... a crisis, it is [the crisis is] the real unchained, impossible to control."[71]

In all other moments, when our financial apparatus has not been paralyzed, a universal fiction makes full use of the above categories. Further, these devices have an uncanny ability to construct a specific type of person - a subject that not only believes in money's powers but *knows* it.[72] Jacques continues:

"The financial universe is an architecture made of fictions and its keystone is what Lacan called a 'subject supposed to know', to know why and how. The crisis is one of trust; and it will last till the subject supposed to know is reconstructed."[73]

This argument has been transposed several times over. Fundamentally, a monetary bound society is strictly about faith, confidence, and belief in a fiction of value. But what this final clarification displays is that everyday people do not operate as if they have bought into or excepted such a fiction. Instead the

---

71. Jacques, 2008, *Financial.*
72. Jacques has a simple statement for what a final crisis tells us about money: "What do we see in this moment of truth about the financial crisis we are in? That it is worthless; that money is like shit!" [Jacques, 2008, *Financial.*]
73. Some may suspect that the use of the world "till" is colloquial or lowbrow - that it is not a world for an academic work. Jacques-Alain Miller is a rigorous thinker and intellectual and has the authority to use this world. [Jacques, 2008, *Financial.*]

ubject operates as if the fiction of value is a truth - a reality and a act. This is what is meant by the "subject is suppose to know"; the ubject is presumed to live as if these fictions are truths and to *now* that money *can* value any object.

So, when Mr. Fuld says "we could not convince the world" ie is making two statements. First, that he could not sustain the iction that his assets under management were as valuable as the price point assigned to them. And second, and more importantly, Mr. Fuld is proclaiming that the subject no longer knows - that the subject lost faith in the fiction of value he worked so hard to offer is a truth.

Appendix

Akerlof, G. A., & Shiller, R. J. (2009). *Animal Spirits: How Human Psychology Drives the Economy, and Why It Matters for Global Capitalism*. Princeton, NJ: Princeton University Press.

Arrighi, G. (1994). *The Long Twentieth Century: money, power, and the origins of our times*. London: Verso.

Ayres, C. (1949). The Value Economy. In R. Lepley (Ed.), *Value: A Cooperative Inquiry* (pp. 43-63). New York: Columbia University Press.

Baudrillard, J. (1975). *The Mirror of Production*. St. Louis: Telos Press.

Baudrillard, J. (1993). *Symbolic Exchange and Death* (H. Grant, Trans.). London: Sage Publications.

Baudrillard, J., & Poster, M. (2001). *Selected Writings*. Stanford: Stanford University Press.

Calomiris, C. W., & Gorton, G. (2000). The Origins of Banking Panics: Models, Facts and Bank Regulation. In C. W. Calomiris (Ed.), *U.S. Bank Deregulation in Historical Perspective* (pp. 93-163). Cambridge: Cambridge University Press.

Cecco, M. D. (1975). *Money and Empire: The International Gold Standard, 1890-1914*. Totowa, N.J: Rowman and Littlefield.

Comaroff, J., & Comaroff, J. L. (2000). Millennial Capitalism: First Thoughts on a Second Coming. In *Public Culture* (pp. 291-343). North Carolina: Duke University Press.

Cottarelli, C., & Giannini, C. (1997). *Credibility Without Rules? Monetary Frameworks in the Post-Bretton Woods Era*. Washington, D.C.: International Monetary Fund.

Critchley, S. (2009, August 30). Coin of Praise. *The New York Times*.

D'Arista, J. W. (1994). *The Evolution of U.S. Finance* (2nd ed.). Armonk, N.Y.: M.E. Sharpe.

Davidson, P. (2006). Exogenous Versus Endogenous Money: The conceptual foundations (M. Setterfield, Ed.). In *Complexity, endogenous money and macroeconomic theory essays in honour of Basil J. Moore*. Northampton, MA: Edward Elgar Pub.

Dean, J. (2008). *Democracy and Other Neoliberal Fantasies: Communicative Capitalism and Left Politics* (1st ed.). Durham: Duke University Press.

Derrida, J. (1980). *Writing and Difference* (A. Bass, Trans.). Chicago: University o Chicago Press.

Derrida, J. (1985). *Margins of Philosophy*. New York: University of Chicago Press.

Derrida, J. (2006). *Specters of Marx*. New York, NY: Routledge.

Engels, F. (1972). *The Origin of the Family, Private Property and the State*. New York: International.

Fisher, I. (1922). *The Purchasing Power of Money Its Determination and Relation to Credit Interest and Crises*. New York: The Macmillan Company.

Fisher, I. (1928). *The Money Illusion*. New York: Adelphi Company.

Foucault, M. (1980). *Power/Knowledge: selected interviews and other writings, 1972-1977*. New York: Pantheon Books.

Foucault, M. (1994). *The Birth of the Clinic*. New York: Vintage Books.

Friedman, M. (1966). *Essays in Positive Economics*. New York: University of Chicago Press.

Friedman, M. (1974). A Theoretical Framework for Monetary Analysis. In R. J. Gordon (Ed.), *Milton Friedman's Monetary Framework: a debate with his critics* (pp. 1-62). Chicago: University of Chicago Press.

Friedman, M. (1992). *Money Mischief: Episodes in Monetary History*. New York: Harcourt Brace Jovanovich.

Friedman, M. (2008). *Milton Friedman on Economics Selected Papers*. New York: University of Chicago Press Journals.

Friedman, M., & Schwartz, J. (1963). *A Monetary History of the United States 1867-1960* (A study by the National Bureau of Economic Research, New York). Princeton: Princeton University Press.

Fuld, R. S., & Gregory, J. M. (2007). *Lehman Brothers Annual Report 2007* (Annual Financial Report). New York: Lehman Brothers.

Goux, J. (1990). *Symbolic Economies: After Marx and Freud* (J. C. Gage, Trans.). Ithaca: Cornell University Press.

Graeber, D. (2001). *Toward an Anthropological Theory of Value: The False Coin of Our Own Dreams*. New York: Palgrave Macmillan.

Grasso, S. (Narrator). (2010, February 4). *Word on the Street, Fast Money*. Live performance in the Nasdaq Market Site, New York City.

Greider, W. (1987). *Secrets of the Temple: How the Federal Reserve Runs the Country* (1st ed.). New York: Simon & Schuster.

Harvey, D. (2006). *Limits to Capital*. London: Verso.

Heilbroner, R. L., & Smith, A. (1987). *The Essential Adam Smith*. New York: W.W. Norton.

Ho, K. (2009). *Liquidated: An Ethnography of Wall Street*. Durham: Duke University Press.

House Financial Services committee Hearing on Lehman Bros Report, 111th congress Cong. (2010) (testimony of Richard, S. Fuld, Jr).

Innes, M. A. (2004). *Credit and State Theories of Money: The Contributions of A. Mitchell Innes* (R. L. Wray, Ed.). Cheltenham, UK: Edward Elgar.

Kemmerer, E. W. (1919). *The ABC of the Federal Reserve System* (3rd ed.). London: Princeton University Press.

Keynes, J. M. (1930). *A Treatise on Money* (1st ed., Vol. 1). London: Macmillan Limited.

Keynes, J. M. (1991). *The General Theory of Employment, Interest, and Money* (New ed.). San Diego, CA: Harcourt, Brace, Jovanovich.
    Original Publication Year: 1936.

Kupiec, P. H., & Ramirez, C. D. (2008, April). *Bank Failures and the Cost of Systemic Risk: Evidence from 1900-1930* (Working paper No. 1421885). Retrieved November 1, 2009, from Federal Deposit Insurance Corporation website: http://ssrn.com/abstract=1421885

Lemos, R. M. (1995). *Nature of Value Axiological Investigations*. Gainesville: University Press of Florida.

Lerner, E. M. (1954). The Monetary and Fiscal Programs of the Confederate Government, 1861-1865. *Journal of Political Economy*, 506-522.

LiPuma, E. (2004). *Financial Derivatives and the Globalization of Risk (Public Planet)*. New York: Duke University Press.

Mackenzie, D. (2008). *An Engine, Not a Camera: How Financial Models Shape Markets*. Cambridge: The MIT Press.

Marx, K. (1935). *Value, Price and Profit*. USA: International.

Marx, K. (1981). *Capital Volume I* (B. Fowkes, Trans.). London: Penguin Books.
    Original Publication Year: 1867.

Marx, K. (2000). *Selected Writings* (D. McLellan, Ed.). Oxford; New York: Oxford University Press.

Marx, K. (2009). *A Contribution to the Critique of Political Economy*. Ithaca, NY: Cornell University Library.
    Original publication Year: 1859.

Mauss, M. (2006). *The Gift: The Form and Reason for Exchange in Archaic Societies* (2nd ed.). New York: Routledge.

Mckay, P. A. (2010, February 17). Dow Rallies 169.67 as View Brightens. *The Wall Street Journal*.

Meltzer, A. H., & Greenspan, A. (2004). *A History of the Federal Reserve, Volume 1 1913-1951* (1st ed., Vol. 1). New York: University of Chicago Press.

Miller, J. A. (2008, October 20). The Financial Crisis [Editorial]. *Lacan.com*.

Minsky, H. P. (1975). *John Maynard Keynes*. New York: Columbia University Press.

Minsky, H. P. (2008). *Stablizing an Unstable Economy*. New York: McGraw-Hill.

National Mining Association. (2008). [The History of Gold]. Unpublished raw data.

Nelson, A. (2002). *Marx's Concept of Money: The God of Commodities* (2nd ed.) New York: Hobbs the Printers.

Office of the Curator. (2006). *The History of the Department of the Treasury* (Rep.). Washington: Department of the Treasury.

Orszag, P. (2007). *Estimated Costs of U.S. Operations in Iraq and Afghanistan and of Other Activites Related to the War on Terrorism* (United States of America, Congressional Budget Office). Washington: Congressional Budget Office.

Plato. (2007). *The Republic* (H. D. Lee & M. S. Lane, Trans.). London: Penguin Books.

Porter, M. (Ed.). (2009). *Financial Crises: a detailed view on financial crises between 1929 and 2009* (1st ed.). Hamburg, Germany: MLP.

Potter, D. M. (1976). *The Impending Crisis: 1848-1861*. New York: Harper & Row.

Preda, A. (2009). *Framing Finance*. Chicago: University of Chicago Press.

Rich, F. (2009, October 17). Goldman Can Spare You a Dime. *The New York Times*.

Simmel, G. (1903). *The Metropolis and Mental Life*. Dresden: Petermann.

Simmel, G. (1978). *Philosophy of Money* (1st ed.). London: Routledge & Kegan Paul.

> This is the first complete English translation of the revised edition (1907) of Georg Simmel's work "Philosophie des Geldes," which was first published in 1900.

Smithin, J. (Ed.). (2000). *What Is Money?* New York: Routledge.

Steinherr, A. (1998). *Derivatives: The Wild Beast of Finance*. New York: Wiley.

The Board of Governors of The Federal Reserve System. (2005). *The Federal Reserve System Purposes & Functions*. Washington: Publications Department.

The Process of Exchange. (1981). In K. Marx (Author) & B. Fowkes (Trans.), *Capital Volume I* (pp. 178-187). London: Penguin Books.

> Original Publication Year: 1867.

Truth and Power. (1980). In M. Foucault (Author), *Power/knowledge selected interviews and other writings, 1972-1977*. New York: Pantheon Books.

Twain, M. (1898). *Following the Equator: A Journey Around the World*. American Publishing Company.

Vilar, P. (1976). *A History of Gold and Money 1450-1920* (J. White, Trans.). London: Atlantic Highlands: Humanities Press.

World Official Gold Holdings - September 2009 (Rep.). (2009). London: World Gold Council.

Wray, R. L. (1998). *Understanding Modern Money: The Key to Full Employment and Price Stability*. Cheltenham: Edward Elgar.

Made in the USA
Columbia, SC
26 March 2021